Also by Hugh Carpenter and Teri Sandison

Hot Wok
Hot Chicken
Hot Pasta
Hot Barbecue
Hot Vegetables
The Great Ribs Book

Fast Appetizers

Hugh Carpenter
and Teri Sandison

TEN SPEED PRESS
Berkeley, California

Ten Speed Press
Post Office Box 7123
Berkeley, California 94707
www.tenspeed.com

Distributed in Australia by Simon & Schuster Australia, in Canada by Ten Speed Press Canada,
in New Zealand by Southern Publishers Group, in South Africa by Real Books, in Southeast
Asia by Berkeley Books, and in the United Kingdom and Europe by Airlift Book Company.

Cover and book design by Beverly Wilson
Typography by Laurie Harty

Library of Congress Cataloging-in-Publication Data
Carpenter, Hugh.
Fast Appetizers/written by Hugh Carpenter & Teri Sandison; photography by Teri Sandison.
    p.   cm.
ISBN 1-58008-049-9
1. Appetizers. 2. Cookery, International. 3. Quick and easy cookery. I. Title.
TX740.C313 1999
641.8'12--dc21   99-20151
                        CIP

First printing, 1999
Printed in Hong Kong

6 7 8 9 10 — 03 02

We dedicate this book with love to our sisters and brothers: Barbara, Jud, Bonnie, and Janet. Gather your family and friends and enjoy these fast appetizers. We're on our way over!

Contents

Fast Appetizers for Every Occasion

*H*ere are fast appetizers for every occasion, to begin a worknight meal or a holiday gathering, to usher in an evening of romance or a reunion of college friends, to eat alone or with your family. These appetizers will reverse flagging spirits, excite the appetite, stimulate conversation, and provide a welcome change from the day's activities.

Little bites of intense flavor heighten anticipation for the main entrée. Pick appetizers that vary dramatically in color, texture, and taste.

Emphasize the contrasts by choosing appetizers from different cuisines. Heighten their visual appeal by garnishing with sprigs of herbs, edible flowers, and twists of thinly sliced citrus.

Tease, tempt, and torment your dinner guests. Limit appetizers to 2 or 3 choices, even for large dinners. Serve highly flavored little nibbles that intensify but never overwhelm everyone's hunger. Follow the standard catering formula of 3 portions per person per appetizer.

Keep all the appetizers bite-size so these nibbles are consumed using your fingers or with toothpicks. This way appetizer forks, plates, and cleanup are minimized.

If time is especially limited, make use of ready-to-serve appetizers such as those listed in Fast Appetizers from Everyday Pantry Items, or choose from the fastest recipes in the book, which are found in the following chapters: Fantastic Dips and Spreads, Bar Food Nibbles, and Crudités for Small Parties and Crowds.

Get your guests involved adding toppings to pizza or folding dumplings. A little culinary activity adds a sense of spontaneity to the beginning of a party and provides a congenial setting to reaffirm old ties and begin new friendships.

These fast appetizers use flavor combinations from around the world to create intense, exciting flavors. Enter the kitchen now and make a few of these recipes. Watch your guests as they crowd ever closer to the appetizers. Have a culinary adventure and let these recipes play a starring role for your family and friends every night.

Hugh Carpenter and Teri Sandison

Menu Planning

Are the appetizers for a dinner party?

*I*f the dinner party includes a substantial entrée, serve no more than 3 appetizers and limit the quantity of each appetizer to 2 to 3 portions or bites per person. If the appetizers are the main focus of the dinner, serve 3 to 6 choices, each appetizer serving 3 to 5 portions or bites per person.

Are you comfortable having friends in the kitchen lending a helping hand?

*T*he completion of a few of the recipes is greatly speeded by friends helping. We've found that most people love a little culinary activity. If so, choose one appetizer from one of the following chapters: Sizzling Appetizers from the Grill and Oven, New Ideas for Pizzas, Out of the Wok in Seconds, or Asian Dumplings and Spring Rolls.

Do you want to serve appetizers that need minimal preparation?

*C*hoose from Fantastic Dips and Spreads, Bar Food Nibbles, Fast Appetizers from Everyday Pantry Items, and Crudités for Small Parties and Crowds.

Do you want to minimize your time spent on last-minute cooking?

*C*hoose any of the cold appetizers or any hot appetizer from Meatball Appetizers East and West, Flaky Pastry Packages, and Quick Tex-Mex Appetizers. You can make them in advance and simply heat up to serve.

Do you want to serve appetizers that can be prepared more than 24 hours in advance?

Many recipes in this book fall within this category, including recipes from Fantastic Dips and Spreads, Perfect Pâtés in Minutes, Cured Meats and Seafood, Flaky Pastry Packages, Asian Dumplings and Spring Rolls, and many recipes in Quick Cheese Appetizer Wonders.

Are you giving an appetizer party?

If so, serve one or more of the following substantial appetizers: Tuscan-Style Chilled Salmon, Asian Smoked Salmon with Ginger and Sesame, Chinese Chicken Wings, Beef Tenderloin in Our Favorite Barbecue Sauce, Pork Baby Back Ribs, and any of the recipes from the chapters New Ideas for Pizzas or Quick Tex-Mex Appetizers. If you're serving grilled beef, a salmon fillet, sliced ham, or a cheese platter, accompany with sliced bread or little rolls, mustards, and dips, so guests can engineer their own sandwiches.

Do you want the appetizers to have an ethnic theme?

Most of the recipes in this book are Mediterranean. But there are plenty of options for an Asian party, too. Choose recipes from the following chapters: Asian Dumplings and Spring Rolls; Out of the Wok in Seconds; Sushi, Sashimi, and New World Rolls; Sizzling Appetizers from the Grill and Oven; and individual recipes such as Spicy Thai Meatballs Wrapped with Lettuce, Chilled Shrimp with Basil Ponzu Sauce, Asian-Smoked Salmon with Ginger and Sesame, and Thai Shrimp Pizza. For Southwestern-Mexican, choose from the chapter Quick Tex-Mex Appetizers and individual recipes such as Tuna and Scallop Ceviche, Barbecued Oysters with Chipotle-Lime Butter, Spicy Southwest Meatballs with Sharp Cheddar and Pine Nuts, New Age Guacamole, Thai Tomato Salsa, Mexican Warm Cheese Dip, Ancho Chile Dip, Spicy Avocado and Goat Cheese Dip, and Chilled Southwest Scallops.

Shortcuts in the Kitchen Everyone Should Know

Mincing Ginger

Do not peel ginger unless the skin is wrinkled. Wash and dry. Cut the ginger crosswise (never lengthwise) into paper-thin slices. Stand the slices on their edge in a garlic press, then press the plunger down, or mince in an electric mini-chopper.

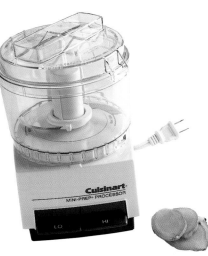

Peeling and Mincing Garlic

Press the garlic, skin on, through the garlic press, or peel and mince in an electric mini-chopper.

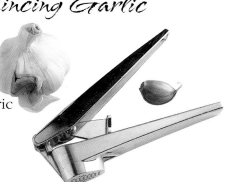

Grating Citrus Zest

Use the citrus grater called the "Great Zester" as shown.

Juicing Citrus

Extract small amounts of juice most quickly by using a wooden reamer (not a plastic reamer) or a small juicer.

Mincing Green Onions

Double the green onion back and forth, then mince. Or, tear into small pieces and drop down the feed tube of a food processor while the machine is on.

Mincing Herbs

Bunch the herbs under your fingers, then cut thinly and finish by mincing. Do not mince in an electric mini-chopper or food processor because the blade tears and blackens the leaves.

Grating and Shredding Cheese

Grate hard cheeses using a hand grater or grating wheel, or cut into small pieces and drop down the feed tube of a food processor while the machine is on. Shred soft cheeses using a hand grater or the shredding blade of a food processor.

Roasting Peppers

Place on a gas stovetop flame turned to the highest setting or under an electric broiler. When the pepper turns black, rotate the pepper one-third of a turn. Continue turning and, when completely blackened, seal in a plastic or paper bag for 5 minutes, then rub off the black skin.

Removing Silver Skin from Salmon and from Beef Tenderloin

Place the salmon or tenderloin, silver skin side down, on a cutting board. Grasp the edge of the silver skin and, making very small cutting motions, cut the meat off the silver skin.

Shelling and Deveining Shrimp

To save preparation time, always buy large shrimp, at least 15 to 20 to a pound, or bigger. Cut along the top ridge (opposite the leg side) and remove the vein.

Clarifying Butter

Melt butter over low heat; remove the butter solids that float to the top with strips of paper towel.

Toasting Sesame Seeds

Place in an ungreased skillet over high heat. Shake the pan. When shaking the pan, prevent sesame seeds from escaping by placing a lid on the pan.

Piping Pâtés and Cheese Mixtures

Use a cloth pastry bag lined on the inside with plastic and various sizes of decorative tips.

Pitting Olives

The best olive pitters we've found are the Westmark and Pedrini models.

Grinding Spices

Use an electric coffee grinder that is reserved just for this purpose.

Fast Appetizers from Everyday Pantry Items

*L*ocal supermarkets, delicatessens, and gourmet shops provide many premade foods that are perfect fast appetizers. Here are some of our favorites, which, when necessary, are provided with serving ideas. We have not included any "dips," "snacks," "party treats," or other heavily processed, artificially seasoned, and phony colored "foods." May they remain forever unsold.

To Serve with Crackers

*E*xcept for the cheese, the following foods can be placed on crackers that are lightly buttered or spread with cream cheese and garnished with chopped parsley or cilantro.

Any premium domestic or imported cheese

Tapenades, such as mushroom, olive, and artichoke

Any thinly sliced smoked or barbecued meats from the deli counter

Caviar, both refrigerated and from the shelf

Anchovies packed in oil

Smoked oysters

Sardines

Smoked salmon, sold by the slice in the deli section (not prepackaged)

Smoked trout sold in the deli section

Canned and fresh pâtés

To Use for Dips and to Toss with Chilled Shrimp

Fresh salsas, sold refrigerated (purchase within 5 days of being made)

Red pepper dipping sauce

Chutneys

Flavored oils

Barbecue sauces

To Serve Alone as Finger Food or with Toothpicks

Spicy pickles

Bottled chiles, such as jalapeño peppers

Cornichons (gherkins in vinegar)

Stuffed olives, with chiles, anchovies, almonds, and pimientos

Pitted kalamata olives

French niçoise olives

Dried Greek olives

Marinated artichoke hearts

Smoked almonds

Honey-roasted peanuts

Roasted salted hazelnuts

Macadamia nuts

Tortilla chips, both plain and flavored

To Wrap Around Melon Slices or Chilled Cooked Asparagus

Any thinly sliced cured meat from the deli counter, such as

Fire-roasted New York steak

Genoa salami

Pepper salami

Prosciutto

Country ham

Maple-honey turkey

Black Forest ham

Smoked chicken

Smoked turkey

Fantastic Dips and Spreads

*W*hat differentiates dips from spreads is their consistency. Dips are liquid concoctions into which other ingredients are briefly plunged. Spreads, as their name implies, are thick enough to be spread on crackers and sandwiches, or to form a thick coating on an ingredient such as chilled asparagus. Both add a special taste to many appetizers. Use these dips and spreads to add zest to chilled cooked shrimp and other seafood, as a flavoring for blanched chilled vegetables, to glaze crisp deep-fried wontons and spring rolls, to drizzle over skewers of barbecued meat and seafood, or simply to serve with tortilla chips. Any of the following dips made with yogurt or sour cream can be changed into a spread by replacing the yogurt or sour cream with an equal amount of cream cheese.

Spicy Chunky Peanut Dip

MAKES 1½ CUPS

½ cup chunky peanut butter
¼ cup dry sherry
2 tablespoons honey
2 tablespoons white or red wine vinegar
2 tablespoons flavorless cooking oil
1 tablespoon dark sesame oil
1 tablespoon soy sauce
1 teaspoon Asian chile sauce
2 cloves garlic, finely minced
2 tablespoons finely minced ginger
2 tablespoons finely minced green onion

*I*n a small bowl, combine all of the ingredients until well blended. If necessary, thin the dipping sauce by stirring in a few teaspoons of cold water. Store in the refrigerator. *The dip will keep for up to 1 week in the refrigerator.*

Jade Dip

MAKES 1 1/2 CUPS

2 cups spinach leaves
1/4 cup fresh cilantro
8 leaves fresh basil
8 leaves fresh mint
2 cloves garlic, chopped
1 tablespoon finely minced ginger
1/3 cup freshly squeezed orange juice
1/4 cup plain yogurt
2 tablespoons white or red wine vinegar
1 tablespoon dark sesame oil
1 tablespoon hoisin sauce
1/2 teaspoon Asian chile sauce

*P*lace all of the ingredients in a blender and liquefy. Refrigerate. *The dip will keep for up to 2 days in the refrigerator.*

Sweet-and-Sour Apricot Dip

MAKES 3 CUPS

See photographs, pages 79 and 105.

15 dried apricots
1 3/4 cups apricot nectar
1/2 cup sugar
1/2 cup distilled white vinegar
1 teaspoon Asian chile sauce
1 tablespoon minced ginger

*I*n a small saucepan over high heat, combine all of the ingredients. Bring to a boil, reduce heat to low, cover, and simmer for 30 minutes. Remove from the heat and let cool. Place in a blender and liquefy. *The dip will keep for up to 6 months in the refrigerator.*

Thai Tomato Salsa

MAKES 2 CUPS

See photograph, page 65.

1 1/2 cups seeded and chopped vine-ripened tomatoes
2 tablespoons chopped fresh cilantro
1 tablespoon finely minced ginger
3 tablespoons freshly squeezed lime juice
2 tablespoons light brown sugar
2 tablespoons Thai or Vietnamese fish sauce
2 teaspoons Thai or other Asian chile sauce

*I*n a small bowl, combine all of the ingredients. Serve at room temperature or chilled. *The salsa will keep for up to 2 days in the refrigerator.*

Mango or Papaya Salsa

MAKES 1¾ CUPS

See photograph, page 105.

2 tablespoons chopped green onions
2 tablespoons chopped fresh cilantro
1 tablespoon finely minced ginger
1 cup chopped mango or papaya flesh
3 tablespoons freshly squeezed lime juice
2 tablespoons light brown sugar
2 tablespoons Thai or Vietnamese fish sauce
    or low-sodium soy sauce
½ teaspoon Asian chile sauce

*I*n a small bowl, combine all of the ingredients. *The salsa will keep for up to 12 hours in the refrigerator.*

Mexican Warm Cheese Dip

MAKES 2 CUPS

8 ounces mild Cheddar or Monterey jack cheese, shredded
    (about 2 cups)
3 ounces cream cheese, cut into small pieces
½ cup whipping cream
½ cup canned diced green chiles
1 tablespoon hot sauce
1 clove garlic, finely minced
4 cups tortilla chips, as accompaniment

*P*lace all of the ingredients except the chips into a small saucepan. *The recipe can be completed to this point up to 8 hours before heating.* Place the pan over low heat and warm the dip, stirring constantly, until the cheese is melted. Be careful not to let it boil, or the oil will separate from the cheese. Taste and adjust for spiciness. Transfer to a warm serving bowl. A lighted Sterno can underneath will keep it warm as long as needed. Serve at once with chips.

Blue Cheese Dip with Smoked Almonds

MAKES 2 CUPS

4 slices bacon, browned and crumbled
2 cloves garlic, finely minced
8 ounces cream cheese, cut into small pieces
4 ounces blue cheese, crumbled
¼ cup half-and-half
2 tablespoons chopped chives
3 tablespoons chopped smoked almonds

*I*n a saucepan combine the bacon, garlic, cream cheese, blue cheese, and half-and-half. *The recipe can be completed to this point up to 8 hours before heating.* Place the pan over low heat and warm the dip, stirring constantly, until the cheese is melted. Stir in the chives. Transfer to a warm serving bowl that has a lighted Sterno can under it to keep the dip warm. Sprinkle with the chopped almonds. Serve.

From left: Mango or Papaya Salsa, Mexican Warm Cheese Dip, Blue Cheese Dip with Smoked Almonds

Aioli Dipping Sauce

1 cup mayonnaise (not lowfat)
1 (7-ounce) jar roasted red peppers, drained and minced
4 cloves garlic, finely minced
2 teaspoons freshly squeezed lemon juice
Dash ground white pepper

In a small bowl, combine all of the ingredients. Keep refrigerated. *The dip will keep for up to 4 days in the refrigerator.*

Roast Garlic Spread

MAKES 1¼ CUPS

1 head roasted garlic (page 28)
8 ounces cream cheese, cut into small pieces
2 to 4 tablespoons heavy whipping cream
2 tablespoons chopped chives

Squeeze the garlic cloves from their skins. Place the garlic, cream cheese, and cream in a food processor. Process until smooth. *The dip will keep in the refrigerator for up to 3 weeks.* Sprinkle the spread with chives and serve at room temperature.

Spicy Avocado and Goat Cheese Dip

MAKES 2 CUPS

2 avocados, seeded, skinned, and mashed
4 ounces soft goat cheese, crumbled
1 tablespoon freshly squeezed lime or lemon juice
2 cloves garlic, finely minced
2 serrano chiles, seeds included, minced
¼ cup chopped fresh cilantro sprigs
½ teaspoon salt

In a bowl, combine all of the ingredients and mix well. *The dip will keep for up to 2 days in the refrigerator.*

Chipotle Chile Dip

MAKES 1⅓ CUPS

2 tablespoons canned chipotle chiles in adobo sauce
1 cup sour cream
2 tablespoons heavy whipping cream
2 tablespoon freshly squeezed lime juice
2 cloves garlic, finely minced
2 tablespoons chopped fresh mint or cilantro sprigs

Finely mince the chiles in a food processor. Add all of the remaining ingredients except the herbs and process until smooth. Transfer the dip to a bowl, stir in the herbs, and refrigerate. *The dip will keep for up to 5 days in the refrigerator.*

Roasted Eggplant Dip

MAKES 1½ CUPS

1 large globe eggplant
¼ cup extra virgin olive oil
2 cloves garlic, finely minced
¾ cup sour cream
½ teaspoon salt
½ teaspoon crushed red pepper flakes

Preheat the oven to 350°. Cut the eggplant into ½-inch slices. Rub with the oil and garlic. Place on a baking sheet and roast in the oven until very soft, about 30 minutes. Transfer to a food processor and purée. Transfer to a bowl, and stir in all of the remaining ingredients. *The dip will keep for up to 3 days in the refrigerator.*

Tapenade Spread

MAKES ¾ CUP

1 cup pitted imported black olives, such as kalamata
1 tablespoon minced oil-packed anchovies
1 clove garlic, finely minced
½ teaspoon freshly ground black pepper
1 teaspoon grated lemon zest
¼ cup extra virgin olive oil

Place all of the ingredients in a food processor and purée. Transfer to a bowl and refrigerate. *The dip will keep for up to 2 weeks in the refrigerator.*

Roasted Red Pepper Dip

MAKES 2¼ CUPS

See photograph, page 23.

8 sundried tomatoes
1 clove garlic, finely minced
1 tablespoon finely minced ginger
14 ounces bottled roasted red peppers, drained
1 tablespoon freshly squeezed lemon or lime juice
2 tablespoons chopped chives
4 ounces cream cheese
½ cup sour cream
1 teaspoon ground coriander
½ teaspoon Asian chile sauce or hot sauce
Chopped red bell pepper, as garnish
Chopped chives, as garnish

Place the sundried tomatoes in a small bowl and cover with boiling water. Let sit for 20 minutes, then drain. Mince the garlic in a food processor. Add the ginger, tomatoes, and red pepper and finely mince. Add all of the remaining ingredients and process until smooth. Garnish with the chopped red pepper and chives. *The dip will keep for up to 5 days in the refrigerator.*

Spicy Cocktail Dip

MAKES 1 CUP

1 cup taco sauce, such as La Victoria Red Taco Sauce
Juice from 1 lime
1 teaspoon hot sauce, or more to taste
2 tablespoons chopped fresh cilantro sprigs
1 clove garlic, finely minced

In a small bowl, combine all of the ingredients. *The dip will keep for up to 3 days in the refrigerator.*

Ancho Chile Dip

MAKES 2 CUPS

3 ancho chiles
1 cup sour cream
$1/_4$ cup white or red wine vinegar
$1/_4$ cup flavorless cooking oil
$1/_4$ cup light brown sugar
2 cloves garlic, finely minced
1 tablespoon finely minced ginger
$1/_2$ teaspoon ground cumin

P lace the chiles in a small bowl and cover with boiling water. Let sit for 20 minutes, then drain. Stem and remove the seeds. Mince the chiles in a food processor. Add all of the remaining ingredients and process until smooth. *The dip will keep for up to 5 days in the refrigerator.*

New Age Guacamole

MAKES 1 $1/_2$ CUPS

2 ripe avocados, seeded, skinned, and mashed
$1/_2$ cup chopped jicama
2 tablespoons minced green onions, white and green parts
1 tablespoon minced fresh cilantro sprigs
$1/_2$ teaspoon finely minced garlic
1 tablespoon freshly squeezed lemon juice
1 teaspoon Asian chile sauce or hot sauce
$1/_4$ teaspoon salt
1 sprig cilantro, as garnish

I n a bowl, combine all of the ingredients and mix well. Press plastic wrap across the surface and refrigerate. *The dip will keep for up to 12 hours in the refrigerator.*

From left: Ancho Chile Dip, New Age Guacamole, Roasted Red Pepper Dip (page 21)

Bar Food Nibbles

Little, intensely flavored bites, usually heavily spiced and salted, are a favorite nibble at bars. However, any two or three of the following recipes are all that's necessary to serve as appetizers preceding a dinner. Extraordinarily simple and requiring little or no last-minute attention, these also make an ideal choice for large gatherings. Recipes for the other classic bar food, nachos, are found on pages 90–91.

Spicy Peanuts

MAKES 2 CUPS

See photograph, page 27

2 cups raw peanuts, shelled and papery skins rubbed away
1 cup peanut oil
1 teaspoon salt
$\frac{1}{2}$ teaspoon cayenne pepper, or more to taste

P lace the nuts and oil in a 2$\frac{1}{2}$-quart saucepan. Cook over medium-high heat, stirring, until the nuts turn a very light golden brown, about 2 minutes. Immediately tip the nuts and oil into a sieve placed over another saucepan. Discard the oil and transfer the nuts to paper towels to dry. Sprinkle while still hot with the salt and cayenne pepper. When cool, transfer the nuts to a plastic bag and freeze. *This recipe can be completed to this point up to 3 months before serving.* Serve at room temperature.

Olives with Chiles, Garlic, and Herbs

MAKES 3 CUPS

See photograph, page 27.

3 cups imported green or black olives, pitted
$\frac{1}{4}$ cup extra virgin olive oil
2 tablespoons balsamic vinegar
2 tablespoons chopped fresh basil
2 cloves garlic, finely minced
$\frac{1}{2}$ teaspoon grated orange zest
$\frac{1}{2}$ teaspoon grated lemon zest
$\frac{1}{2}$ teaspoon crushed red pepper flakes

I f olives are in a marinade, then drain. In a bowl, combine the olives and all of the other ingredients. Stir well. Marinate at room temperature for 12 hours or refrigerate. *This recipe can be completed to this point up to 3 days before serving.* To serve, drain thoroughly. Serve at room temperature.

Barbecued Spicy Sausages

SERVES 4 TO 8

¹/₂ pound fresh spicy sausage
One or more dipping sauces (pages 16–22)

Preheat a gas barbecue or indoor grill to medium (350°) or, if using charcoal or wood, prepare a fire and let it burn until the coals or wood are ash-covered. Grill the sausages until firm and fully cooked in the center. Cool to room temperature. Cut into ¹/₄-inch-thick slices and serve or refrigerate. *The recipe can be completed to this point up to 24 hours before serving.* Serve with a dipping sauce and toothpicks.

Stuffed Grapes Rolled in Crushed Pecans

SERVES 4 TO 6

¹/₂ cup pecans
20 large seedless grapes
2 ounces blue cheese, crumbled

Preheat the oven to 325°. Spread the pecans on a baking sheet and toast in the oven until dark, about 15 minutes. Let cool, then finely chop in a food processor.

Using the end of a bamboo skewer, create a funnel-shaped opening at the top end of each grape. Fill each with about 1 teaspoon blue cheese. Roll the cheese end of the grape in the chopped pecans. Refrigerate. *The recipe can be completed to this point up to 24 hours before serving.* Serve chilled or at room temperature.

Rosemary Walnuts

MAKES 2 CUPS

2 ¹/₂ tablespoons unsalted butter
2 teaspoons dried rosemary
1 teaspoon salt
¹/₂ teaspoon cayenne pepper
2 cups walnuts

Preheat the oven to 350°. Place the butter in a 12-inch sauté pan over medium heat. When the butter sizzles but has not browned, add all of the remaining ingredients. When the nuts are evenly coated, transfer to a baking sheet lined with parchment paper. Place the nuts in the oven and bake until golden brown, about 10 minutes. Leave the nuts on the pan and let cool to room temperature. Transfer to a zip-top bag and store in the freezer. *This recipe can be completed to this point up to 3 months before serving.* To serve, transfer to a bowl and serve at room temperature.

Spicy Olives

2 cups imported green or black olives, pit in or pitted
1 tablespoon California chili powder or your favorite
    chili powder

*I*f olives are in a marinade, then drain. In a bowl, stir the olives and chili powder until evenly mixed. Serve or refrigerate. *The recipe can be completed to this point up to 2 weeks before serving.* Serve at room temperature.

Olives Stuffed with Goat Cheese and Chiles

SERVES 6 TO 12

4 ounces soft goat cheese, at room temperature
1 tablespoon chopped chives
$^1/_2$ teaspoon crushed red pepper flakes
20 large imported olives, pitted

*I*n a small bowl, combine the goat cheese, chives, and pepper flakes and mix until smooth. Place in a pastry bag fitted with a medium pastry tip. Pipe about 1 teaspoon of the goat cheese into the olives. Refrigerate until ready to serve. *The recipe can be completed to this point up to 4 days before serving.* Serve at room temperature.

Spicy Candied Pecans

MAKES 1 POUND

1 pound shelled pecans or walnut halves
$^1/_4$ cup honey
$^1/_4$ cup sugar
$^1/_4$ cup water
$^1/_2$ teaspoon crushed red pepper flakes
$^1/_2$ teaspoon salt

*P*reheat the oven to 325°. In a medium saucepan over high heat, bring 2 quarts water to a boil. Add the nuts and boil for 2 minutes. Drain. Meanwhile, in a $2^1/_2$-quart saucepan over medium-high heat, combine all of the remaining ingredients. Bring to a low boil. Transfer the nuts, while still piping hot, into the honey-sugar mixture. Increase the heat to high and stir the nuts until all the liquid disappears.

Spread the nuts on a baking sheet lined with parchment paper. Place the nuts in the oven and bake until they become a dark mahogany color, about 20 minutes (using a spatula, turn the nuts over halfway through the cooking process). Leave the nuts on the pan and let cool to room temperature.

When cool, separate the nuts and place them, still on the baking sheet, into the freezer. When frozen, transfer to a zip-top bag and store in the freezer. *The recipe can be completed to this point up to 3 months before serving.* To serve, transfer the nuts to a bowl and serve frozen.

From left: Olives with Chiles, Garlic, and Herbs (page 24), Olives Stuffed with Goat Cheese and Chiles, Spicy Candied Pecans, Spicy Peanuts (page 24)

Artichoke Hearts with Chiles, Garlic, and Balsamic Vinegar

SERVES 6 TO 10

2 (6½-ounce) jars marinated artichoke hearts, drained
2 cloves garlic, finely minced
1 teaspoon finely minced fresh rosemary
½ teaspoon crushed red pepper flakes
2 tablespoons balsamic vinegar
2 tablespoons extra virgin olive oil

Cut the artichoke hearts in half and transfer to a bowl. Add all of the remaining ingredients. Stir well and refrigerate. *The recipe can be completed to this point up to 1 week before serving.* To serve, bring to room temperature. Place on a serving plate and serve with toothpicks or skewers.

Roasted Garlic

MAKES 4 HEADS

4 large heads garlic
¼ cup extra virgin olive oil
Salt to taste
Crackers or thinly sliced baguette, toasted, or Jumbo Chile
    Cilantro Croutons (at right) as accompaniment

Preheat the oven to 400°. With a sharp knife, cut off and discard the tips from the garlic heads. Place on a layer of aluminum foil and drizzle the oil over the exposed garlic cloves. Fold the foil over the garlic heads and seal so it becomes an airtight envelope. Place the garlic in the oven and roast for 1 hour. Let cool. Remove from the foil and leave at room temperature for up to 12 hours, or refrigerate. *The recipe can be completed to this point up to 2 weeks before serving.*

To serve, if the garlic is refrigerated, bring to room temperature. Sprinkle with salt. Each person removes a garlic clove and, by pressing the skin, squeezes the garlic paste onto a cracker or baguette slice.

Jumbo Chile Cilantro Croutons

MAKES 4 CUPS

8-inch baguette or bread, sweet or sour
½ cup extra virgin olive oil
6 cloves garlic, finely minced
1 teaspoon crushed red pepper flakes
½ teaspoon salt
¼ cup chopped fresh cilantro sprigs

Preheat the oven to 350°. Cut the bread into ⅛-inch slices. In a small sauté pan over medium-high heat, combine the oil and garlic. Heat until the garlic begins to sizzle but has not turned brown. Remove from the heat and stir in the red pepper flakes and salt. Brush the sliced bread on both sides with the oil mixture. Transfer the bread to a baking sheet. Place in the oven and bake until golden brown, about 15 minutes. Transfer to a baking pan lined with paper towels and let cool. When cool, transfer to a zip-top bag and freeze. *The recipe can be completed to this point up to 3 months before serving.* To serve, bring the croutons to room temperature and sprinkle with the cilantro.

*From top: Roasted Garlic.
Jumbo Chile Cilantro
Croutons, Artichoke Hearts
with Chiles, Garlic,
and Balsamic Vinegar*

Crudités for Small Parties and Crowds

While they take only minutes to prepare, the varying shapes, colors, textures, and subtle flavors of vegetables provide an ideal introduction to a meal—and they won't dull the anticipation for the courses to follow. Offer even the most modest selection, such as carrot sticks to dip in a salt-and-pepper blend, and you'll be amazed how they disappear. Whatever combination of vegetables you serve, plan on a total of 5 pieces per person. Follow the easy vegetable preparation steps outlined in this chapter and make one or more dipping sauces. With all the time you'll save, go play!

Vegetables to Serve Raw

Vegetables that can be served whole, such as baby radishes, thin green beans, or tiny mild peppers, only need trimming. Cut larger ones like carrots, celery, yellow squash, zucchini, or jicama into "sticks."

Grilled and Roasted Vegetables

Grilled and roasted vegetables taste sensational. The hot, dry heat from the grill or oven intensifies the unique flavors, concentrates the natural sugars, adds a deep low-note taste, and gives vegetables a bold, rustic look. Before cooking, brush the vegetables with extra virgin olive oil, an oil-and-vinegar salad dressing, or your favorite marinade. Cook the vegetables until they brighten in color, are well heated through, have lost their raw taste, and have light char marks. Vegetables cook quickly, so turn them frequently and brush often with extra marinade. Serve all grilled vegetables hot or at room temperature. Do not try to keep them warm or reheat them. *The vegetables can be prepared up to 4 hours before serving.*

Blanched Chilled Vegetables

Blanching, an ideal cooking technique for preparing hard-textured vegetables to be served chilled or at room temperature, means to quickly cook food in a large quantity of boiling water, just until it is crisp-tender.

To blanch, trim and cut the vegetables into the desired size. Bring enough water to a rapid boil to allow the vegetables to "swim." Drop in the vegetables. Since the cooking process is very quick, stir the vegetables continuously. The moment the vegetables turn a bright color and are tender, drain them in a colander, and then immediately plunge them into a bowl of cold water and ice. When the vegetables are chilled, pat them dry and refrigerate until ready to use. Serve all blanched vegetables cold from the refrigerator. *The vegetables can be blanched up to 12 hours before serving.*

Vegetables to Grill, Roast, or Blanch

Asparagus

Snap off and discard the tough stems. Grill for about 2 minutes on each side, depending on the size. Or blanch until bright green, 15 to 30 seconds, then chill in ice water.

Baby Beets

Roast in a 400° oven until tender, about 20 minutes.

Broccoli

Discard tough ends, peel stems, and cut between florets to separate. Blanch just until tender, about 2 minutes, then chill in ice water.

Carrots

Peel carrots. Cut large carrots into sticks lengthwise and grill about 2 minutes on each side or skewer baby carrots and grill for about 2 minutes on each side.

Cauliflower

Break into individual florets. Grill for about 10 minutes on each side until tender. Or blanch just until tender, about 1 minute, then chill in ice water.

Eggplant

Cut Japanese or Chinese eggplant lengthwise into 3 strips. Brush with an oil-and-vinegar salad dressing. Marinate 15 minutes. Grill for about 2 minutes on each side.

Green Beans

Trim tough stem ends. Skewer and grill for about 6 minutes on each side. Or blanch just until tender, about 2 minutes, then chill in ice water.

Mushrooms

Choose firm mushrooms (button, cremini, portobello, shiitake, porcini, chanterelles, and morels), not soft ones (oyster or enoki). Discard tough ends. Either grill the mushrooms whole and then slice, or slice and place on bamboo skewers. Brush with oil or a marinade. Grill until the mushrooms soften slightly, about 6 minutes. Serve hot or at room temperature with toothpicks.

Peppers

Stem, seed, and remove the ribs. Grill for about 4 minutes on each side. Cut into long strips about $\frac{1}{2}$ inch wide.

Caviar for Special Occasions

From the most expensive caviar flown in from the Caspian Sea to the inexpensive lumpfish caviar sold unrefrigerated by most supermarkets, each type has its place in home entertaining.

Premium fresh caviar is now produced in the United States, but the best kinds are still beluga, osetra, and sevruga caviar from Iran and Russia, sold at fine-food markets in refrigerated tins. Unopened and refrigerated, caviar will keep for up to 6 weeks. But once opened, it is highly perishable and should be eaten within a week.

Crostini with Brie and Caviar

SERVES 6 TO 10

Here's a wonderful caviar crostini. Do all the preparation hours in advance and then assemble the appetizer just before your dinner guests arrive.

16 ($^1/_4$-inch-thick) slices baguette
6 cloves garlic, peeled and split in half
$^1/_4$ cup extra virgin olive oil or unsalted butter
16 thin slices Brie, Camembert, or any triple-cream cheese (about $^1/_3$ pound)
2 hard-boiled eggs, chopped
2 ounces fresh black, golden, or red caviar
2 tablespoons minced fresh cilantro, parsley, or chives
2 teaspoons grated lemon zest

Preheat the broiler to 400°. Arrange the baguette slices on a baking sheet and toast under the broiler until lightly golden on each side, about 1 minute. Rub each side of the toast with garlic and then brush one side very lightly with olive oil. Place the prepared crostini in an airtight container and store at room temperature until serving. *The recipe can be completed to this point up to 8 hours before serving.*

To serve, place a slice of cheese on the oiled side of each crostini. Add a sprinkling of the egg, then the caviar, cilantro, and lemon zest. Transfer the crostini to a serving platter and serve.

Easy Caviar Dip

SERVES 8 TO 12

This is a very easy and delicious recipe using the inexpensive black caviar sold in glass jars at most markets. While you can substitute moderately expensive fresh caviar, don't use very expensive fresh caviar, whose subtle, complex flavor will be overwhelmed by the other ingredients.

3 tablespoons mayonnaise
6 hard-boiled eggs, chopped
1 1/2 cups chopped red onion
8 ounces cream cheese, at room temperature
2/3 cup sour cream
1 (4-ounce) jar black lumpfish caviar
Crackers, thinly sliced baguette, or endive cups, as
    accompaniments

In a small bowl, stir together the mayonnaise and the hard-boiled eggs. Spread the mixture over the bottom of an 8-inch springform pan. Layer the onion on top. Combine the cream cheese and sour cream, and spread evenly over the onions. Sprinkle with the caviar. Refrigerate. *The recipe can be completed to this point up to 2 days before serving.*

To serve, remove the sides of the springform pan. Transfer the bottom of the pan to a round serving plate. Serve chilled with crackers, baguette slices, or endive cups.

Baby Red Potatoes with Caviar Thrones

SERVES 8 TO 12

It's the contrasts of black against white, starchy sweetness versus the slight ocean briny taste, and the soft texture accenting the little crunchy topping that makes potatoes and caviar an ideal combination. See photograph, pages 34–35.

20 baby red potatoes, or 8 to 10 small red potatoes
2 tablespoons flavorless cooking oil
2 ounces fresh caviar, good to best quality
2 tablespoons chopped fresh chives

Preheat the oven to 375°. Rub the potatoes with the oil. Place them on a sheet pan and roast in the oven until they feel tender when prodded with a fork, about 30 minutes. Cool to room temperature.

Using a paring knife, cut a tiny section off the bottom of each potato so that it will sit upright when served. Cut a little hole in the top of each potato. Fill with caviar and sprinkle with chives. As an option, you can also make an X on the potato, squeeze the potato slightly, and then place caviar on the top. Refrigerate. *The recipe can be completed to this point up to 8 hours before serving.* Serve chilled.

Fresh Caviar and Its Garnishes

No appetizer is more luxurious, better appreciated, and easier to present than fresh caviar. The best way to appreciate caviar is simply to place a small spoonful on the soft skin stretching between your thumb and index finger, gently lift the caviar off with your tongue or offer your hand to a friend, and follow with a fine Champagne. For an elaborate party presentation, serve fresh caviar—about 2 ounces for every 6 people—with small bowls of one or more of the following:

¹/₂ cup sour cream
¹/₄ cup chopped hard-boiled egg whites
¹/₄ cup chopped hard-boiled egg yolks
¹/₄ cup chopped red onion
2 tablespoons finely chopped chives
Lemon wedges
Thinly sliced buttered toast points, crusts removed

*P*lace the opened tin of caviar in a glass bowl filled with crushed ice and insert a tiny demitasse spoon. Place the accompaniments in little dishes around the caviar

From left: Fresh Caviar and Its Garnishes, Baby Red Potatoes with Caviar Thrones (page 33)

Quick Cheese Appetizer Wonders

*F*ine cheese is one of life's great taste sensations. In this chapter you'll find ten enticing cheese appetizers. The easiest appetizer choice is simply an assortment of cheeses. However, cheese is so rich that it can quickly overwhelm the appetite and ruin any enthusiasm for the dinner to follow.

If you want to serve a cheese unadorned by other flavors, limit yourself to one choice and pick a more aggressive-tasting cheese such as Stilton or sharp Cheddar, or serve a cheese course after the main entrée. On the other hand, for large gatherings, few appetizers are more appreciated by those gathered, and by the cook, than a cutting board holding a magnificent display of cheeses.

Prosciutto Cheese Wraps

SERVES 4 TO 8

This fast recipe can be assembled hours in advance. Use any top-quality cheese, vary the herbs by replacing the basil with cilantro or mint, or add thinly sliced imported olives.

3 very thin slices prosciutto, about 1½ ounces
¼ pound Brie, blue cheese, or goat cheese
¼ cup bottled roasted red peppers
16 very small basil leaves

*T*rim off all the fat along the edges of the prosciutto. Cut into 16 strips measuring ½ inch wide by 4 to 5 inches long. Cut the cheese and the red pepper into 16 pieces. Roll one piece of cheese, one piece of pepper, and a basil leaf with a strip of prosciutto. Secure with a toothpick. Repeat with remaining pieces. Refrigerate. *The recipe can be completed to this point up to 12 hours before serving.* Serve chilled or at room temperature.

Lettuce-Wrapped Spicy Goat Cheese

SERVES 4 TO 10

Lettuce leaves hiding a complex-tasting cheese filling make an intriguing presentation. For variation, try serving this goat cheese in endive cups or on apple slices or crackers.

4 ounces soft goat cheese
2 tablespoons pine nuts
1 ear white corn (optional)
2 tablespoons minced bottled roasted red pepper
2 tablespoons dried currants
2 tablespoons chopped fresh cilantro
1/2 teaspoon hot sauce
1 clove garlic, finely minced
1/4 teaspoon salt
4 large leaves Bibb lettuce

Preheat the oven to 325°. Place the goat cheese in a mixing bowl. Place the nuts on a baking sheet and toast in the oven until golden, about 8 minutes. Cut the kernels off the corn. Add the nuts, pepper, corn, currants, cilantro, hot sauce, garlic, and salt to the goat cheese and, using your hands, mix thoroughly. Divide the mixture into 16 equal pieces. Using your fingers, roll each piece into a 1½-inch cylinder. Discard the ribbing from the lettuce and cut each leaf into 4 pieces. Wrap each piece of goat cheese with a leaf and refrigerate. *The recipe can be completed to this point up to 24 hours before serving.* Serve chilled.

Fragrant Goat Cheese with Roasted Garlic

SERVES 4 TO 10

Here's another fast appetizer that is packed with lots of flavor. If you don't have time to roast the garlic, just gently rub the goat cheese with a raw garlic clove that has been spilt in half, then discard the garlic and add the other seasonings.

1 (6-ounce) log soft goat cheese
2 teaspoons roasted garlic (page 28)
2 teaspoons freshly ground black pepper
1 teaspoon grated orange zest
2 tablespoons minced fresh basil
2 tablespoons minced fresh mint
1 tablespoon white sesame seeds, toasted
Crackers or endive cups, as accompaniment

Place the goat cheese on a serving plate. Gently rub the surface of the cheese with the roasted garlic, then evenly sprinkle the remaining ingredients except the crackers or endive cups over it. Serve or refrigerate. *The recipe can be completed to this point up to 24 hours before serving.* Serve at room temperature with crackers or endive cups.

Marinated Goat Cheese with Garlic, Basil, and Orange Zest

SERVES 6 TO 10

It's the infused olive oil that gives the goat cheese an intense and exciting flavor. You can vary the type of peppercorns used, or substitute mint or cilantro for the basil. This marinated goat cheese is also very good served in Belgian endive cups. See photograph, page 38.

1 (12-ounce) log soft goat cheese, or 3 smaller logs, chilled
³/₄ cup extra virgin olive oil
1 tablespoon whole peppercorns, preferably a mixture of white, red, and black
1 teaspoon whole allspice berries
2 cloves garlic, finely minced
2 tablespoons finely minced fresh ginger
¹/₃ cup slivered fresh basil
1 teaspoon grated orange zest
Crackers, as accompaniment

Using a thin-bladed vegetable knife or paring knife, cut the goat cheese into ¹/₂-inch-thick slices. (Dip the knife blade in hot tap water after each cut.) Arrange the slices in a single layer in a Pyrex pie plate or baking dish.

In a small saucepan, combine the olive oil, peppercorns, and allspice. In a small bowl, combine the garlic, ginger, basil, and orange. Place the saucepan over medium-high heat and cook until the peppercorns begin to pop, about 2 minutes. Remove the pan from the heat and immediately stir in the garlic mixture. After 5 seconds of stirring, pour the hot olive oil mixture over the goat cheese. Marinate in the refrigerator at least 3 hours, covered with plastic wrap. *The recipe can be completed to this point up to 1 week before serving.*

To serve, transfer the chilled cheese to a serving plate. Serve at room temperature or chilled with crackers.

Brie Baked with Black Pepper and Toasted Pecans

SERVES 6 TO 12

We think baked Brie tastes so much more exciting when its surface is layered with toasted nuts and cracked pepper. It's also great with Our Favorite Barbecue Sauce (page 72), a storebought tapenade, or spicy jalapeño jelly. Addicting!

¹/₄ cup pecans
1 (9-ounce) round Brie or Camembert cheese
2 teaspoons freshly cracked black pepper
1 teaspoon grated orange zest
Thinly sliced bread, crackers, apple or pear slices, or endive cups, as accompaniment

Preheat the oven to 325°. Place the pecans on a baking sheet and toast in the oven until golden, about 15 minutes. Let cool, then finely chop. Using your fingers, rub the pepper, orange zest, and pecans on all sides of the Brie. Refrigerate. *The recipe can be completed to this point up to 24 hours before cooking.*

Preheat the oven to 250°. Bake the brie until it is warm throughout, about 10 minutes, but has not melted. Serve immediately with sliced bread, crackers, apple or pear slices, or endive cups.

Hot Pepper Jelly Cheesecake

SERVES 4 TO 8

Here's another very simple recipe. Try varying the nuts and herbs—but not the pepper jelly!

$^1/_4$ cup pine nuts
8 ounces cream cheese, at room temperature
1 cup hot pepper jelly, preferably red
2 cloves garlic, finely minced
$^1/_4$ cup chopped fresh cilantro
5 ounces sharp Cheddar cheese, grated (about $1^1/_4$ cups)
Sliced bread, crackers, or Belgian endive cups, as accompaniment

Preheat the oven to 325°. Place the pine nuts on a baking sheet and toast in the oven until golden, about 8 minutes. Set aside.

Place the cream cheese, $^1/_2$ cup of the jelly, garlic, cilantro, and Cheddar cheese in a food processor. Process until evenly blended. Line the bottom of a 7-inch springform pan with parchment paper. Spray the sides of the pan with nonstick spray. Add the cheese mixture. Refrigerate for at least 2 hours. Spread the remaining jelly evenly across the top surface and sprinkle on the pine nuts. *The recipe can be completed to this point up to 24 hours before serving.*

To serve, carefully remove the sides of the pan. Transfer the cheesecake to a serving plate. Serve chilled with sliced bread, crackers, or endive cups.

Grilled Figs Stuffed with Blue Cheese

SERVES 4 TO 8

The sharp blue cheese, sweet warm figs, complex pancetta, and brush of sweet-sour balsamic vinegar all conspire to create an alluring rainbow of flavors.

12 small figs, not quite ripe
$^1/_4$ pound blue cheese, any type, crumbled
$1^1/_2$ ounces thinly sliced pancetta, prosciutto, or country ham
$^1/_4$ cup balsamic vinegar

Cut the figs in half only halfway, cutting from the top down. Stuff with about 1 tablespoon of the blue cheese. Wrap each fig with a slice of pancetta, securing the pancetta with a toothpick. Refrigerate. *The recipe can be completed to this point up to 24 hours before cooking.*

Preheat a gas barbecue or indoor grill to medium (350°) or, if using charcoal or wood, prepare a fire and let it burn until the coals or wood are ash-covered. Brush the grill with oil. Place the figs on the grill and brush with some of the balsamic vinegar. Cook the figs for about 30 seconds on each side, until they are just heated through. Brush on more balsamic vinegar. Serve at once.

Apricot Thrones with Cheese and Pecans

SERVES 6 TO 10

This is one of the fastest recipes in the book. It's also excellent using just Brie cheese instead of cream cheese and blue cheese.

15 pecan halves
2 ounces cream cheese, at room temperature
2 ounces blue cheese
15 dried apricots

Preheat the oven to 325°. Place the pecans on a baking sheet and toast in the oven until golden brown, about 15 minutes.

Combine the cheeses and stir until evenly mixed. Divide the cheese mixture into 15 equal pieces. Place 1 piece of cheese on top of each apricot and top with a toasted pecan. Transfer the apricots to a serving plate and refrigerate. *The recipe can be completed to this point up to 8 hours before serving.* Serve at room temperature.

Endive Cups Filled with Cheese, Mango, and Toasted Pecans

SERVES 6 TO 12

Belgian endive cups are a perfect appetizer container to hold cheese because their slight bitterness is nicely offset by the richness of the filling. See photograph, page 43.

$1/4$ cup pecans
$1/2$ small ripe mango, or $1/4$ cup storebought mango chutney
1 tablespoon finely minced ginger
1 teaspoon Asian chile sauce or hot sauce (optional)
4 ounces cream cheese, at room temperature
18 large leaves Belgian endive (about 4 large heads), chilled

Preheat the oven to 325°. Place the pecans on a baking sheet and toast in the oven until golden brown, about 15 minutes. Then cool to room temperature and coarsely chop.

If using fresh mango, peel the mango, cut the flesh away from the seed, and coarsely chop the flesh. In a bowl, combine the nuts, mango, ginger, chile sauce, and cheese. Using your hands, mix evenly. Refrigerate. *The recipe can be completed to this point up to 8 hours before serving.*

No more than 2 hours before serving, fill the endive cups. Place the filled endive cups on a serving plate and serve.

Warm Apricots Stuffed with Blue Cheese and Walnuts

SERVES 10 TO 20

Teri and I enjoyed this appetizer at Napa Valley's famous Mustards Restaurant in June 1990. The recipe is very simple, elegant, and utterly delicious, but it does require good tree-ripened apricots.

15 fresh tree-ripened apricots
Juice of 1 lemon
$\frac{1}{3}$ cup walnut pieces
$\frac{1}{2}$ pound blue cheese
$1\frac{1}{2}$ ounces thinly sliced country ham
3 cups baby spinach leaves or arugula leaves
1 tablespoon extra virgin olive oil

Preheat the oven to 325°. Cut the apricots in half and pit. Drizzle the lemon juice over the cut apricot sections. Place the walnuts on a baking sheet and toast in the oven until golden, about 15 minutes. Coarsely chop the walnuts and mix with the blue cheese until evenly combined. Fill the hollow of each apricot half with the mixture. Wrap each apricot half with a single layer of the country ham, securing the ham with a toothpick. Refrigerate. *The recipe can be completed to this point up to 8 hours before cooking.*

Toss the spinach leaves with the olive oil, then place the spinach in an even layer on a serving plate. Grill or broil the apricots. If broiling, preheat the broiler. Place the apricots under medium heat until the cheese just begins to melt, 30 to 60 seconds. If grilling, preheat a gas barbecue or indoor grill to medium (350°) or, if using charcoal or wood, prepare a fire and let it burn until the coals or wood are ash-covered. Brush the grill with oil. Place the apricots on the grill and cook until the cheese just begins to melt, 30 to 60 seconds.

Place the apricots on top of the spinach leaves and serve at once.

From left: Warm Apricots Stuffed
with Blue Cheese and Walnuts,
Endive Cups Filled with Cheese, Mango,
and Toasted Pecans (page 41)

Exciting Chilled Seafood Appetizers

*F*ew appetizers are more appreciated and require less last-minute attention by the home cook than chilled seafood. When pressed for time, purchase chilled, cooked seafood from the local seafood market or from a supermarket whose seafood counter has a good reputation for offering the freshest seafood. Whether you serve large shrimp with a dipping sauce (pages 16-22), a mound of cracked crab, or one of the following recipes, you'll have time to enjoy your guests—and the appetizers.

Tuscan-Style Chilled Salmon

SERVES 12 TO 20

A whole barbecued salmon fillet makes an impressive appetizer. Accompany it with very thinly sliced bread, mustard, and one or more dipping sauces (pages 16–22). Each person can cut a small portion of salmon and assemble his or her own little (or not so little!) open-faced sandwich. For flavor variation, substitute one of the barbecue sauces (pages 72–73) for the Tuscan Marinade.

TUSCAN MARINADE
$1/4$ cup extra virgin olive oil
1 tablespoon grated lemon zest
$1/3$ cup freshly squeezed lemon juice
2 tablespoons honey
$1/4$ cup pitted kalamata olives, minced
2 tablespoons chopped fresh rosemary or fresh basil
2 tablespoons anchovy paste
1 teaspoon crushed red pepper flakes

1 (3-pound) salmon fillet, skin on but pin bones
*   removed by the market*
2 lemons, cut into paper-thin slices
$1/4$ cup chopped fresh parsley
1 teaspoon grated orange zest
1 teaspoon grated lemon zest
Thinly sliced baguette, as accompaniment
Mustard, as accompaniment
One or more dipping sauces (pages 16-22), as accompaniment

*I*n a small, nonreactive bowl, whisk together the marinade ingredients. Marinate the salmon for 30 minutes.

Preheat a gas barbecue or indoor grill to medium (350°) or, if using charcoal or wood, prepare a fire and let it burn until the coals or wood are ash-covered. Brush the grill with oil. Lay the salmon, skin side down, on the grill. Spoon any extra marinade over the salmon. Cover the barbecue with the lid and cook the salmon, without removing the lid, for 15 minutes. Remove the lid and cut into the salmon to check for doneness. It should be slightly undercooked in the center. If you don't want to barbecue, then broil the salmon by placing the fillet 4 inches beneath the broiler heat. Slide two large spatulas under the salmon between the fillet and skin, and carefully transfer the salmon in one piece to a serving platter. Serve hot or, if serving cold, refrigerate at least 2 hours. *The salmon can be prepared up to 8 hours before serving.*

To serve, place a layer of the lemon slices down the center of the grilled salmon. Sprinkle the salmon evenly with the parsley, orange zest, and lemon zest. Serve with baguette slices, mustard, and dipping sauce.

Cajun-Asian Tuna Carpaccio

SERVES 6 TO 10

Here is a good example of fusing ingredients from different cuisines to achieve a new, intensely flavored statement. Be sure to buy bright-red, fresh tuna.

1 pound tuna fillet, sashimi grade
1/4 cup chopped fresh parsley
2 tablespoons grated lemon zest
2 tablespoons capers, rinsed and drained

CAJUN-ASIAN SAUCE
1 cup mayonnaise
1 tablespoon freshly squeezed lime juice
1 tablespoon Grand Marnier
1 tablespoon finely minced fresh ginger
1 teaspoon Worcestershire sauce
1 teaspoon Louisiana Hot Sauce or Asian chile sauce
1 teaspoon minced fresh cilantro
1/2 teaspoon finely grated orange zest

*U*sing a very sharp, thin-bladed knife, cut the fish into 1/4 by 1/2 by 1 1/2-inch pieces (keeping the knife blade wet helps prevent the fish from tearing). Arrange the fish on a serving platter, cover with plastic wrap, and refrigerate.

In a small bowl, combine all of the sauce ingredients, mix well, and refrigerate. *The recipe can be completed to this point up to 8 hours before serving.*

To serve, place about 1 teaspoon of the sauce in the center of each piece of tuna. Sprinkle on the parsley, lemon zest, and capers. Serve at once.

Chilled Shrimp with Basil Ponzu Sauce

SERVES 6 TO 10

Ponzu sauce, a Japanese dipping sauce, begins with soy and citrus juice. The flavors should be sweet, sour, and slightly spicy, with no one flavor dominating. Try substituting freshly squeezed tangerine or grapefruit juice for the lime, or using cilantro instead of basil. This recipe provides a fail-safe technique for cooking shrimp. Follow the boiling and icing procedure, whisk together the Basil Ponzu Sauce, or instead choose another flavorful dip (pages 16–22). Experiment!

1 pound raw medium to large shrimp

BASIL PONZU SAUCE
2 tablespoons thin or low-sodium soy sauce
2 tablespoons freshly squeezed lime juice
2 tablespoons freshly squeezed orange juice
2 tablespoons light brown sugar
2 tablespoons flavorless cooking oil
1/2 teaspoon Asian chile sauce
1 tablespoon finely minced ginger
1 clove garlic, finely minced
1/4 cup chopped fresh basil

*S*hell and devein the shrimp (leaving the tail attached). Bring 4 quarts of water to a rapid boil and add the shrimp. Cook the shrimp until done, about 1 minute (to test, cut a shrimp in half; it should be white in the center). Drain the shrimp in a colander and transfer immediately to a large bowl of ice water. When chilled, drain and refrigerate until ready to use. In a small, nonreactive bowl, combine the sauce ingredients and mix well. If not using right away, refrigerate. *The recipe can be completed to this point up to 10 hours before serving.*

To serve, toss the shrimp with the sauce. Transfer to a serving platter or a decorative bowl and serve immediately.

Spicy Marinated Mussels

SERVES 6 TO 10

These mussels are addicting. Be sure to buy mussels that are tightly closed, and buy a few extra, since there are always a few mussels that do not open. Do not marinate the mussels more than 2 hours, or the texture of the mussels will become mushy.

18 small mussels
3 tablespoons mild olive oil (not extra virgin)

MARINADE
¼ cup bottled roasted red peppers, chopped
2 tablespoons chopped fresh cilantro, mint, or basil
1 clove garlic, finely minced
1 tablespoon finely minced ginger
3 tablespoons unseasoned Japanese rice vinegar
1 tablespoon dark sesame oil
1 tablespoon flavorless cooking oil
½ teaspoon Asian chile sauce or hot sauce
¼ teaspoon salt

Scrub the mussels vigorously and pull away the beards and any seaweed between the shells. In a 4-quart pot, bring 1 inch of water to a vigorous boil. Add the mussels and cover the pot. Cook until the mussels open, about 3 minutes. Discard any mussels that do not open. Transfer the mussels to a colander, let cool, then refrigerate for 1 hour.

In a small, nonreactive bowl, whisk together the marinade ingredients and refrigerate. Carefully remove the mussel meat from the shells; place in a bowl and refrigerate. Open the mussel shells wide, but do not detach the halves. Place the shells in a large bowl, toss with the olive oil until evenly coated, and refrigerate. *The recipe can be completed to this point up to 8 hours before serving.*

To serve, toss the mussels with the marinade. Place a marinated mussel in each shell and arrange on a serving plate.

Chilled Southwest Scallops

SERVES 6 TO 10

It's important to use fresh scallops. Frozen scallops have none of their original beautiful, sweet flavor, and when sautéed they expel all their interior moisture. If fresh scallops are unavailable, substitute large cooked, chilled shrimp.

2 tablespoons flavorless cooking oil
3 cloves garlic, finely minced
½ pound fresh bay scallops
¼ cup pine nuts
1 head Bibb lettuce
1 dried ancho chile
1 whole green onion, minced
¼ cup chopped fresh cilantro
2 tablespoons freshly squeezed lime juice
2 tablespoons brown sugar

In a small bowl, combine the oil and garlic. Place a 12-inch sauté pan over high heat. When very hot, add the oil and garlic. Sauté for a few seconds and then add the scallops. Stir and toss the scallops until they just turn white on the outside, 30 to 60 seconds (they should still be slightly undercooked in the center). Immediately transfer the scallops to a baking sheet. Spread the scallops into a single layer and refrigerate until thoroughly chilled.

Preheat the oven to 325°. Spread the pine nuts on a baking sheet and toast in the oven until golden, about 8 minutes. Set aside. Separate the lettuce leaves, discard the ribs, and tear the leaves into 20 small lettuce cups. Refrigerate. Place the ancho chile in a small bowl, cover with boiling water, and let sit for 30 minutes. Discard the stem and seeds and finely mince. In a small, nonreactive bowl, combine the chile with the green onion, cilantro, lime juice, and sugar, and refrigerate. *The recipe can be completed to this point up to 5 hours before serving.*

Place the chilled scallops in a bowl, add the ancho mixture and pine nuts, and stir well. Serve immediately with the lettuce cups.

Simple Sandwich Starters

*L*ittle sandwiches make a great addition to appetizer parties. The variety of breads and fillings are limitless, and you can save time by trimming and cutting the bread and making the fillings the day before serving. If using a dense bread such as pumpernickel, assemble the sandwiches up to 8 hours in advance. Or, if using a softer type of bread, make the sandwiches no more than 2 hours before serving, to keep the bread from becoming moist.

Some Filling Choices

Cream cheese and freshly ground black pepper

Cream cheese mixed with curry powder

Cream cheese and pepper jelly

Cream cheese, mango chutney, and cilantro sprigs

Cream cheese and roasted red pepper

Cream cheese mixed with chopped fresh mint or cilantro

Cream cheese and thinly sliced imported black or green olives

Cream cheese and thinly sliced cucumber

Thinly sliced cucumber and prepared horseradish

Smoked salmon spread (storebought)

Paper-thin slices of smoked ham and unsalted butter

Caviar and unsalted butter or cream cheese

Watercress and unsalted butter or cream cheese

Chopped hard-boiled eggs mixed with mayonnaise and black pepper

Chopped hard-boiled eggs mixed with capers and Dijon mustard

Blue cheese and unsalted butter

Chicken liver pâté and unsalted butter

Chipotle–Lime Butter (page 69)

Paper-thin slices of roast beef and Our Favorite Barbecue Sauce (page 72)

Goat Cheese–Chive Filling (page 83)

Cranberry and Orange Zest Filling (page 83)

Ginger, Chile, and Goat Cheese Filling (page 83)

Goat Cheese–Peppercorn Filling (page 84)

Some Bread Choices

Baguettes
Black
Brioche
Onion
Potato
Pumpernickel
Rye
White
Whole-wheat

Buy very thinly sliced bread, or thinly slice it with a serrated knife. Stack the sliced bread and cut off the crusts. Seal in a plastic bag and refrigerate. *The bread can be prepared to this point up to 24 hours before serving.*

To assemble, place a very small amount of the filling on a slice of bread. Cover with another piece of bread. If the slices are large, cut in half, into 1-inch-wide rectangles, or into 4 small triangles by cutting corner to corner. If not serving within 30 minutes, place on a tray, cover with plastic wrap, and store at room temperature for several hours. The texture of the sandwich deteriorates if refrigerated.

Perfect Pâtés in Minutes

Spread on crackers or thinly sliced bread, these rich, flavorful pâtés make perfect bites that will tease the palate in anticipation of the main event, or as one of many presentations for an appetizer party. The starting point for creating these delicious pâtés is using fresh chicken livers, unless you're making a vegetarian version. If frozen chicken livers are what's sold by your market, implore the butcher to steal fresh livers from the little bags wedged into the cavities of the whole frying chickens. No one else will know.

Each of the following pâté recipes take just 30 minutes to prepare and can be made days in advance. Best of all, there's no last-minute fuss needed to serve them.

Asian Pâté with Orange Zest

SERVES 6 TO 12

In this recipe, orange zest, chile sauce, and the Chinese seasoning called "five-spice powder" create exciting highlights of flavor and provide the perfect accents to the rich, buttery chicken livers.

$^1/_2$ pound fresh chicken or turkey livers
4 tablespoons unsalted butter
2 cloves garlic, finely minced
2 tablespoons finely minced ginger
1 teaspoon grated orange zest
2 tablespoons oyster sauce
1 teaspoon Asian chile sauce
$^1/_2$ teaspoon sugar
$^1/_4$ teaspoon five-spice powder
3 ounces cream cheese, at room temperature
2 tablespoons Grand Marnier
3 cilantro leaves, as garnish
Crackers or thinly sliced baguette, as accompaniment

Trim the fat from the livers and cut the livers in half. Heat a 12-inch sauté pan over high heat until hot. Add 2 tablespoons of the butter, the garlic, and the ginger. When the butter just begins to brown, add the livers. Stir and toss the livers until they just lose their pink color in the center, about 2 minutes.

Transfer the livers and all pan juices to a food processor. Add the orange zest, oyster sauce, chile sauce, sugar, and five-spice powder and process until completely smooth. Cut the cream cheese and remaining butter into small pieces, then add to the liver mixture. Process until very smooth. Add the Grand Marnier and process again. Transfer the pâté to a serving dish or a 5- to 7-inch tart pan. Press a layer of plastic wrap over the surface. Refrigerate at least 4 hours. *The pâté can be completed to this point up to 5 days before serving.*

To serve, if in a tart pan, remove the sides and transfer the pâté to a round serving plate. Garnish the top with the cilantro. Or, bring to room temperature and transfer the pâté to a small pastry bag fitted with a rose piping tip no larger than #15. Pipe the pâté onto crackers or baguette slices, garnish with the cilantro leaves, and serve at once (or the edges of the pâté will turn a disagreeable, darker color).

Mediterranean Pâté with Olives and Pine Nuts

SERVES 6 TO 12

For true Mediterranean flavor, be sure to use imported black olives, such as the kalamata olives sold at many supermarkets.

¹/₄ cup pine nuts
¹/₃ cup pitted imported black olives
¹/₂ pound fresh chicken or turkey livers
2 tablespoons unsalted butter
4 cloves garlic, finely minced
1 teaspoon fresh thyme
2 teaspoons grated lemon zest
¹/₂ teaspoon salt
¹/₂ teaspoon freshly ground black pepper
4 ounces cream cheese, at room temperature
2 tablespoons Cognac
2 tablespoons chopped fresh chives
Crackers or thinly sliced baguette, as accompaniment

Preheat the oven to 325°. Spread the pine nuts on a baking sheet and toast in the oven until golden, about 8 minutes. Chop the olives.

Trim the fat from the livers and cut the livers in half. Heat a 12-inch sauté pan over high heat until hot. Add the butter and garlic. When the butter just begins to brown, add the livers. Stir and toss the livers until they just lose their pink color in the center, about 2 minutes.

Transfer the livers and all pan juices to a food processor. Add the thyme, lemon zest, salt, and pepper and process until completely smooth. Cut the cream cheese into small pieces, then add to the liver mixture. Process until very smooth. Add the Cognac and process again.

Transfer the pâté to a bowl. Stir in the olives and pine nuts until evenly combined. Transfer the pâté to a serving dish or a 5- to 7-inch tart pan. Press a layer of plastic wrap over the surface. Refrigerate. *The pâté can be completed to this point up to 5 days before serving.*

To serve, if in a tart pan, remove sides and transfer the pâté to a round serving plate. Garnish with the chopped chives. Serve chilled or at room temperature with crackers or baguette slices.

Wild Mushroom Pâté

SERVES 6 TO 12

Although the flavor will be more intriguing if fresh shiitake and chanterelle mushrooms are used, any other firm-textured mushrooms work fine in this pâté, such as fresh button, cremini, portobello, and porcini.

¹/₂ ounce dried cèpes or porcini mushrooms
¹/₄ cup unsalted butter
1 pound fresh firm-textured mushrooms, thinly sliced and
  tough stems discarded
4 cloves garlic, finely minced
2 tablespoons oyster sauce or thin or low-sodium soy sauce
¹/₂ teaspoon hot sauce
¹/₂ teaspoon sugar
6 ounces cream cheese
¹/₄ cup chopped fresh chives, parsley, or cilantro
Crackers or thinly sliced baguette, as accompaniment

*P*lace the dried mushrooms in a small bowl and cover with 1 cup boiling water. Let sit for 30 minutes, then pour the liquid through a fine-meshed strainer. Reserve both the water and the mushrooms.

Heat a 12-inch sauté pan over high heat until hot. Add the butter and, when it begins to brown, add the softened dried mushrooms, fresh mushrooms, and garlic. Sauté until the mushrooms begin to wilt, about 5 minutes. Add the reserved mushroom water, oyster sauce, hot sauce, and sugar. Cook over high heat until all the moisture disappears, about 5 minutes. Remove from the heat and let cool to room temperature.

Transfer the mixture to a food processor and process until smooth. Cut the cream cheese into little pieces, then add it to the mushroom mixture. Process until very smooth. Line the bottom of a 7-inch tart pan with parchment paper and butter the sides. Transfer the pâté to the prepared pan and press a layer of plastic wrap over the surface, or place the pâté in a small decorative bowl. Refrigerate. *The pâté can be completed to this point up to 1 day before serving.*

To serve, remove the sides of the tart pan and sprinkle the pâté with the chopped chives. Transfer the pâté to a round serving plate. Serve chilled or at room temperature with crackers or baguette slices.

Cured Meats and Seafood

*A*ll these recipes can be prepared far in advance and are ideal for large gatherings. If you need more substantial appetizers, you can simply accompany the gravlox, smoked salmon, and beef carpaccio with sliced bread or small rolls, an array of dipping sauces, and baby lettuce greens so your guests can engineer their own tempting sandwiches. Or, if you are pressed for time, purchase smoked salmon, trout, or meat from a delicatessen counter.

Smoked Pork with Ancho Chile Dip

SERVES 6 TO 10

According to food scientist Alan Sams, who teaches at Texas A&M University, meat that is soaked in a brine tastes juicier because the salt penetrates into the muscle, the muscle fibers swell, and the water binds with the protein. This extra moisture is trapped by the meat fiber and isn't lost during cooking. Try brining pork or chicken pieces for 2 hours before barbecuing or roasting. You'll be amazed at the difference in flavor and juiciness.

4 quarts hot water
²/₃ cup salt
1 (12- to 16-ounce) pork tenderloin, silver skin removed by butcher
1 cup Our Favorite Barbecue Sauce (page 72)
Ancho Chile Dip (page 22)
2 tablespoons chopped parsley, chive, or cilantro

*C*ombine the water and salt, and cool to room temperature. Add the pork, submerge it in the water, and refrigerate for 3 hours. Then drain and pat dry. Rub the pork with barbecue sauce. Prepare the Ancho Chile Dip. Smoke the pork, following the directions for smoking on page 57. The pork will be done when its internal temperature reaches 150° on an instant-read meat thermometer, approximately 2 hours in a 200° smoker.

Chill the pork for at least 2 hours, then thinly slice. Place the slices on a decorative plate, cover with plastic wrap, and refrigerate. *The recipe can be completed to this point up to 12 hours before serving.* When ready to serve, top each piece with a little Ancho Chile Dip, garnish with chopped parsley, and serve.

Asian Smoked Salmon with Ginger and Sesame

SERVES 10 TO 20

A whole side of smoked salmon makes a magnificent sight at any gathering. You can smoke the salmon up to 2 days before serving, using a charcoal-fired barbecue with a tight-fitting lid, or by using a charcoal or electric smoker. Unfortunately, unless the manufacturer specifies otherwise, gas grills can't maintain a low enough heat to properly smoke food. Trying to preslice the smoked salmon usually results in badly torn pieces, making an unattractive presentation. Instead, let your guests cut small sections off the salmon.

1 (3-pound) salmon fillet, skin on and pin bones
    removed by the market
¼ cup oyster sauce
¼ cup dry sherry
¼ cup freshly squeezed lemon juice
2 tablespoons dark sesame oil
1 teaspoon Asian chile sauce or hot sauce, or more to taste
¼ cup finely minced ginger
2 whole green onions, finely minced
Crackers or thinly sliced bread, as accompaniment
Lettuce cups, as accompaniment
One or more dipping sauces (pages 16–22), as accompaniment

Place the salmon on a baking sheet with sides. In a small bowl, combine the oyster sauce, sherry, lemon juice, sesame oil, chile sauce, ginger, and green onions. Pour the mixture over the salmon and cover with plastic wrap. Place the salmon in the refrigerator and let it marinate for 1 to 4 hours.

Bring the salmon to room temperature. Soak 2 cups hardwood chips in water for 30 minutes. If using a charcoal-fired barbecue, prepare a fire. If using an electric smoker, preheat to 200°. When the coals are ash-covered, push them to the outside of the smoker. Place a pan of hot water in the bottom of the smoker among the coals. Drain the wood chips and sprinkle half the chips across the coals. Cover the coals with the cooking grate. Lay the salmon, skin side down, in the center of the smoker. Cover the smoker. Regulate the heat so it remains between 180 and 220°. After 45 minutes, add 14 additional charcoal pieces (that have been prelighted) and the rest of the chips.

The salmon is done when it is slightly undercooked in the center, about 1 hour. Transfer the salmon to a baking sheet and refrigerate. When chilled, cover with plastic wrap. *The salmon can be smoked up to 2 days before serving.*

To serve, transfer the salmon onto a serving platter or wooden cutting board. Serve chilled or at room temperature with thinly sliced bread, crackers, or lettuce cups and dipping sauce.

Seared Beef Carpaccio with Lime and Ground Black Pepper

The Italian dish carpaccio is paper-thin slices of raw beef crowned with capers, lemon juice, black pepper, and parsley. This recipe diverges from tradition by searing the beef on the barbecue. The searing makes it easier to slice, and the slightly cooked interior attracts a larger crowd than does a platter of raw beef.

Our Favorite Barbecue Sauce (page 72)
1 1/2 pounds beef tenderloin, trimmed of all fat and silver skin
Juice of 1 lime
Freshly ground black pepper
1 red bell pepper, minced
1/4 cup minced parsley
Crackers, toast points, or lettuce cups, as accompaniments

Brush the barbecue sauce over the meat. Preheat a gas barbecue or indoor grill to medium (350°) or, if using charcoal or wood, prepare a fire and let it burn until the coals or wood are ash-covered. Place the beef on the grill and cook until it reaches an internal temperature of 110° on an instant-read meat thermometer, about 20 minutes. Remove from the grill and refrigerate. *The recipe can be completed to this point up to 24 hours before serving.*

To serve, cut the beef across the grain into very thin slices. This is easier to do if the meat is partially frozen. Place in a single layer on a large serving platter. *The recipe can be completed to this point up to 4 hours before serving, if the surface of the meat is pressed with plastic wrap, then refrigerated.* Just before serving, sprinkle the beef slices with the lime juice, black pepper, minced red pepper, and parsley. Serve with crackers, toast points, or lettuce cups.

Gravlox Infused with Chiles, Cilantro, and Vodka

Gravlox Infused with Chiles, Cilantro, and Vodka

This recipe is a new twist on traditional gravlox. The salmon can be sliced hours before serving. Add leftover gravlox to a green salad tossed with an oil and vinegar dressing for an excellent lunch or dinner entrée. Wrapped in plastic wrap and refrigerated, gravlox will last up to a week.

1 (1-pound) fresh center-cut salmon fillet,
*   silver skin and pin bones removed by market*
Baguette, thinly sliced
1/4 cup unsalted butter, at room temperature
One or more dipping sauces (pages 16–22), as accompaniment
Fresh cilantro sprigs, as garnish

MARINADE
2 to 4 fresh serrano chiles, seeds included, finely minced
4 cloves garlic, finely minced
1/4 cup finely minced fresh ginger
1/4 cup chopped fresh cilantro
1/2 cup vodka
1/4 cup thin or low-sodium soy sauce
1 tablespoon sugar
1 tablespoon salt

Check the salmon for bones and remove any that you find. In a bowl, combine all of the ingredients for the marinade. Place the salmon and marinade in a large plastic zip-top bag. Seal the bag, put it on a tray, and place in the refrigerator. Then place a 5-quart pot filled with cold water on top of the salmon to flatten it and firm its texture (it is unnecessary to turn it). *The salmon must be prepared to this point and allowed to marinate for 2 to 3 days before serving.*

Toast the sliced bread lightly on both sides under the broiler, then lightly butter one side. Prepare a dipping sauce.

With a wet hand, wipe the marinade off both sides of the salmon. Using a very sharp, thin-bladed knife, cut the salmon into about 50 very thin slices, keeping the blade wet so the fish does not tear. Press plastic wrap over the slices so they do not dry out and refrigerate until ready to serve. Place a slice of salmon on each buttered side of bread, then drizzle with sauce and add a cilantro sprig. Serve the salmon chilled.

Swordfish Escabèche with an Asian Twist

SERVES 6 TO 10

Escabèche is a way of curing food, but instead of "cooking" the food using lemon or lime juice as is done for ceviche, heat is first applied, and then the cooked fish is marinated. This technique originated in Spain and is popular throughout Latin America.

1 pound fresh swordfish
Salt and freshly ground black pepper
2 tablespoons olive oil
Aioli Dipping Sauce (page 20)

MARINADE
1 tablespoon finely minced ginger
2 teaspoons grated orange zest
1/4 cup freshly squeezed orange juice
1/4 cup freshly squeezed lemon juice
3 tablespoons extra virgin olive oil
2 tablespoons thin or low-sodium soy sauce
2 tablespoons honey
1 teaspoon hot sauce

Sprinkle both sides of the swordfish with salt and black pepper. Rub the fish with olive oil. Prepare the dipping sauce. In a nonreactive baking pan large enough to hold the swordfish, combine the marinade ingredients and set aside. Preheat a gas barbecue or indoor grill to medium (350°), or, if using charcoal or wood, prepare a fire and let it burn until the coals or wood are ash-covered. Brush the cooking grate with oil and add the fish. Grill the swordfish until it is just slightly undercooked in the center (cut into a piece to check the cooking progress), about 4 minutes on each side. Cool to room temperature. Cut the fish into 1/2-inch-wide strips. Add the strips to the marinade. Cover and refrigerate 2 to 3 hours. Drain the marinade from the fish and return the fish to the refrigerator. *The recipe can be completed to this point up to 8 hours before serving.*

Cut the fish into 1-inch lengths. Arrange the pieces on a decorative platter. Top each piece with a little of the dipping sauce. Sprinkle with parsley and serve.

Tuna and Scallop Ceviche

SERVES 4 TO 8

Although this recipe calls for bay scallops and ahi tuna, you could also use one or more of the following: salmon, sea bass, swordfish, and yellow tail. The secret to ceviche is to use seafood just pulled from the ocean and to match it with assertive flavors such as ginger, cilantro, and chiles. The raw fish is "cooked" by the acidity of the lime juice. If there is any doubt about the freshness of the seafood, choose another appetizer.

1/2 pound fresh bay scallops
1/2 pound ahi tuna
1 cup freshly squeezed lime juice
2 tablespoons finely minced ginger
1 clove garlic, finely minced
2 fresh serrano chiles, seeds included, finely minced
2 tablespoons chopped fresh cilantro sprigs
2 tablespoons flavorless cooking oil
2 tablespoons freshly squeezed orange juice
1/2 teaspoon grated orange zest
1/4 teaspoon salt
Crackers or Belgian endive cups, as accompaniment

Cut the scallops in half. Cut the tuna into the same size pieces as the scallops. Place the scallops and tuna in a nonreactive bowl and add the lime juice. Refrigerate for 4 to 6 hours, stirring occasionally. Prepare and have ready all the remaining ingredients. *The recipe can be completed to this point up to 6 hours before serving.*

Drain the lime juice from the scallops and tuna and discard. Coarsely chop the scallops and tuna, then place in a clean glass bowl. Add all the remaining ingredients except the crackers or endive cups and mix well. Serve or refrigerate 1 to 4 hours before serving. Transfer to a serving bowl. Serve chilled with crackers or endive cups.

Tuna and Scallop Ceviche

Sushi, Sashimi, and New World Rolls

Japanese and Vietnamese-inspired nibbles are an exquisite way to begin a dinner party, even if none of the subsequent food is Asian. The appetizers in this chapter require a little more preparation time and may seem complicated, but actually they come together rather quickly. Three special ingredients—Vietnamese rice paper, Japanese nori, which is thin sheets of dried seaweed, and sushi rice, a special variety of medium-grain rice—are available at many supermarkets and at all Asian markets.

Tuna Sashimi with Wasabi

SERVES 4 TO 8

Sashimi is any kind of raw fish that is thinly sliced and served with soy-wasabi dip. The key to success lies in using only the freshest fish—fish that has arrived at the market the day you are serving it. If you have any doubts about the freshness of the fish, there is a fantastic source for sashimi and sushi—any nearby Japanese restaurant. The afternoon of the party we take a platter into our favorite Japanese restaurant and have the chef place an array of sushi, sashimi, and nori-wrapped "rolls" on the platter. Kept in our refrigerator the rest of the day, these little nibbles, accented by wasabi and pickled ginger, are a fantastic start to our dinner party.

1 pound sashimi-grade raw tuna, bright red in color
3 tablespoons Japanese seasoned rice vinegar
2 tablespoons thin or low-sodium soy sauce
2 to 3 teaspoons powdered wasabi (Japanese horseradish)
1 tablespoon finely minced ginger
2 teaspoons white sesame seeds
1 tablespoon chopped chives or cilantro
1 teaspoon grated lemon zest

Using a very thin, sharp knife, cut the tuna into $1/4$-inch-thick pieces about $1/2$ inch wide and 1 inch long. Dipping the knife in cold water after each slice helps to prevent the fish from tearing. Place the tuna in a single layer on a decorative platter. Press with plastic wrap and refrigerate. In a bowl, combine the vinegar, soy sauce, wasabi, and ginger. Stir well and set aside. In a greased skillet over high heat, toast the sesame seed until light golden. *The recipe can be completed to this point up to 8 hours before serving.*

Stir the wasabi mixture and drizzle over the tuna. Sprinkle the tuna with chives, sesame seeds, and lemon zest. Serve at once.

Nori Rolls with Barbecued Meat

SERVES 4 TO 8

Television cooking teacher Martin Yan made these at a party given to launch his latest PBS cooking show. Since the rolls must be served immediately after they're prepared, they make a great appetizer for a small, casual gathering—but only if your guests feel comfortable assembling their own. The activity will lend a sense of spontaneity that will usher in an evening of fun. This is also excellent using chilled cooked shrimp, smoked salmon, or fresh crab in place of the meat.

1/2 pound boneless country-style spareribs
Our Favorite Barbecue Sauce (page 72)
1/2 cup sushi rice
1/2 cup plus 2 tablespoons cold water
2 tablespoons Japanese seasoned rice vinegar
1/4 cup white sesame seeds
4 sheets nori, each about 7 by 8 inches
2 cups daikon sprouts (radish sprouts)
One or more dipping sauces (pages 16–22)

Trim all excess fat from the meat. Cut the meat into 1-inch-thick strips. Rub the meat on all sides with the barbecue sauce (refrigerate any unused sauce). Barbecue the meat over medium heat until it just loses its pink interior color, about 10 minutes. Remove from the grill and let cool to room temperature. (Alternatively, roast the meat in a 325° oven for about 15 minutes.) Slice the meat into 16 bite-size pieces and refrigerate.

Cook the sushi rice as described on page 66. Then toss with the rice vinegar. Toast the sesame seeds until golden, about 2 minutes. Set aside. (As an option, wave each sheet of nori over the flame of a gas burner for a few seconds in order to crisp it.) Cut the nori in quarters from corner to corner. *The recipe can be completed to this point up to 8 hours before serving.*

To serve, place the meat, rice, sprouts, sesame seeds, nori, and dipping sauce on a serving platter or in little bowls. Have each person take a piece of nori, add a bit of rice, a few sprouts, and a piece of barbecued pork, and then roll it into a little funnel-shaped cone. Top with the sesame seeds and dipping sauce.

Ahi Tuna Summer Rolls

SERVES 6 TO 10

I saw the Beringer Winery executive chef, Jerry Comfort, make these little ahi summer rolls at a food conference. They were a big hit. The only modification here is that we replaced seaweed with daikon sprouts. The key technique is to roll the cylinders tightly. If you can only find smaller rice paper sheets, make individual summer rolls.

3/4 pound fresh ahi tuna fillet, about 6 inches long
1 tablespoon freshly ground black pepper
1 tablespoon flavorless cooking oil
2 tablespoons powdered wasabi (Japanese horseradish)
5 tablespoons water
2 tablespoons white sesame seeds
3 pieces rice paper sheets, 8-inch diameter
1 cup daikon sprouts (radish sprouts)
1/4 cup fresh cilantro sprigs

Cut the tuna into 3 long strips. Rub with the black pepper and then the oil. Preheat a gas barbecue or indoor grill to medium (350°) or, if using charcoal or wood, prepare a fire and let it burn until the coals or wood are ash-covered. Brush the grill with oil. Sear the tuna about 10 seconds on each side and remove it from the heat when still raw in the center. Refrigerate.

In a small bowl, combine the wasabi and water, stirring until well blended. In an ungreased skillet over high heat, toast the sesame seeds until light golden, then set aside. *The recipe can be completed to this point up to 8 hours before serving.*

Within 2 hours of serving: Dip a sheet of rice paper into very hot water and place on a flat surface. Using the back of a spoon or a pastry brush, brush a very thin layer of wasabi over the surface. Sprinkle on one third of the sesame seeds. Along the bottom third of the rice paper, place one third of the sprouts in an even layer. Top with 1 or 2 cilantro sprigs, then a strip of tuna. Tightly roll the rice paper into a cylinder. Repeat with the remaining ingredients. Place the rolls on a baking sheet, cover with wet paper towels, then a layer of plastic wrap, and refrigerate until ready to serve.

To serve, cut the rolls at a sharp angle into 1-inch lengths, making 14 to 18 pieces. Place on a serving platter. Serve immediately.

Vietnamese Summer Rolls

SERVES 6 TO 12

These little cylinders consist of paper-thin Vietnamese rice paper filled with shrimp, mango, and lettuce greens, served uncooked. The thinness and tenderness of rice paper varies, so try the various brands available at your local Asian market and find the thinnest and most tender. We like a brand called Kim Tar Brand from Thailand. Rice paper is always sold unrefrigerated.

16 medium raw shrimp, or ¹/₂ pound fresh crabmeat
1 tablespoon olive oil
1 tablespoon unseasoned Japanese rice vinegar
1 cup baby lettuce leaves, shredded spinach,
    Bibb lettuce, or iceberg lettuce
5 rice paper sheets, 8 inches in diameter
1 cup coarsely chopped mango or papaya
10 fresh cilantro sprigs
2 tablespoons shredded mint leaves
¹/₄ cup chopped unsalted roasted peanuts or pine nuts
One or more dipping sauces (pages 16–22)

Shell and devein the shrimp. Bring 2 quarts of water to a rapid boil and add the shrimp. Cook the shrimp until done, about 1 minute (to test, cut a shrimp in half; it should be white in the center). Drain the shrimp in a colander and transfer immediately to a bowl of ice water. When chilled, drain and pat dry. Split the shrimp in half lengthwise and refrigerate until ready to use.

In a small bowl, combine the oil and vinegar and set aside. To make the rolls, toss the lettuce with the oil and vinegar. Dip a piece of rice paper into hot water and place on a flat surface. When it softens, cut in half with scissors. Place 3 pieces of shrimp end to end about 1 inch from the bottom edge of the paper. Top with 1¹/₂ tablespoons mango, 1 tablespoon lettuce, 1 cilantro sprig, mint shreds, and a sprinkling of nuts. Fold each side of the rice paper over the filling, and tightly toll into a cylinder. Repeat with the remaining ingredients. Place the rolls in a single layer on a baking sheet, cover with a damp dish towel and plastic wrap, then refrigerate. Prepare a dipping sauce. *The summer rolls can be completed to this point up to 2 hours before serving.*

If the rice paper has begun to dry, spray the surface with a little warm water. Cut the summer rolls in half at a slight angle and transfer to a serving platter. Serve chilled with dipping sauce.

Vietnamese Summer Rolls with
Thai Tomao Salsa (page 17)

Smoked Salmon Rolls with Japanese Nori

SERVES 4 TO 8

Years ago, I watched the chefs at the Lodge at Koeli on the Hawaiian island of Lanai make these. If you can't find nori, the Japanese paper-thin seaweed sheets, at your supermarket, ask a Japanese restaurant if they will sell you a few sheets. There is quite a difference in the tenderness of nori depending on the manufacturer, so if you have more than one choice, buy several brands and do a taste test. (We like those made by Sushi Chef.) It's very important to use sushi rice in this recipe. This is a medium-grain Japanese white rice that must not be confused with glutinous rice (also known as sweet rice).

6 paper-thin slices smoked salmon,
    the best quality you can obtain (about 1 ounce)
$1/_2$ cup sushi rice
$1/_2$ cup plus 2 tablespoons cold water
2 tablespoons seasoned Japanese rice vinegar
2 tablespoons powdered wasabi (Japanese horseradish)
5 tablespoons water
3 tablespoons white sesame seeds
3 pieces rice paper sheets, 8 inches in diameter
3 pieces nori, each about 7 by 8 inches
About 12 spinach leaves, stemmed
One or more dipping sauces (pages 16–22)

Keep the salmon refrigerated. Place the rice in a strainer and rinse thoroughly with cold running water. Drain well. Place the thoroughly drained rice in a small saucepan. Add the $1/_2$ cup plus 2 tablespoons cold water and let rest for 60 minutes. Bring the water to a boil over high heat. Stir once, then cover with a lid and reduce the heat to low. Cook 12 to 15 minutes, covered, until the rice is tender. Transfer the rice to a bowl and gently toss with a rubber spatula. Pour the seasoned vinegar over the rice, and then gently toss the rice to coat. (Be careful not to pack or fracture the rice.) Cool to room temperature.

In a small bowl, combine the wasabi and water; refrigerate. In an ungreased skillet over high heat, toast the sesame seeds until golden, about 2 minutes. Set aside. *The recipe can be completed to this point up to 8 hours before serving.*

Within 2 hours of serving: Dip a sheet of rice paper into very hot water and place on a flat surface. Using the back of a spoon or a pastry brush, brush a very thin layer of wasabi over the surface. Place the nori, smooth side up, on the rice paper. (As an option, wave each sheet of nori over the flame of a gas burner for a few seconds in order to crisp it.) Along the bottom third of the nori, place 3 spinach leaves end to end. Using your fingers moistened with water, spread on a thin layer (about $1/_3$ cup) of sushi rice. Top with 2 slices smoked salmon, placed end to end. Tightly roll the rice paper into a cylinder. Place the rolls on a baking sheet, cover with wet paper towels, and refrigerate until ready to serve.

To serve, cut the rolls at a sharp angle into 1-inch lengths, making 14 to 18 pieces. Place on a serving plate. Serve immediately.

Sizzling Appetizers from the Grill and Oven

*M*eats and seafood cooking on the grill or in the oven create an alluring smell that invariably attracts the guests. We make these marinades in large amounts and store them in the refrigerator so that these appetizers are even easier to make. If you want to minimize last-minute attention, try the chicken wing and rib recipes, which can be cooked hours before serving. But if you have good friends who might lend a helping hand, try the Spicy Barbecued Shrimp or any of the skewered foods.

Spicy Barbecued Shrimp
SERVES 4 TO 8

Everyone loves barbecued shrimp. You can serve the shrimp straight from the barbecue, or barbecue the shrimp in advance and serve it chilled.

1 pound large raw shrimp (about 16)
Spicy Asian Marinade (page 73) or one of the other
marinades

*S*hell, devein, and split the shrimp deeply along the top ridge (leaving the tail attached) and refrigerate. *The recipe can be prepared to this point up to 8 hours before cooking.*

Within 30 minutes of cooking, toss the shrimp with the marinade. Preheat a gas barbecue or indoor grill to medium (350°) or, if using charcoal or wood, prepare a fire and let it burn until the coals or wood are ash-covered. Brush the grill with oil, then lay the shrimp on the grill. Grill the shrimp about 90 seconds on each side, brushing on extra marinade as they cook. They are done when they turn pink, feel firm when pressed with your finger, and have turned white on the inside (cut into a shrimp to check). (Or, broil the shrimp under a hot broiler about 1 minute on each side.) Transfer the shrimp to a serving platter. Serve at once, or refrigerate and serve chilled.

Barbecued Oysters with Chipotle-Lime Butter

SERVES 6 TO 12

This delicious and easy recipe from Cakebread Winery chef Brian Streeter just involves barbecuing whole oysters until their shells pop open, and then serving them with a tasty sauce of chipotle, lime, and butter. This sauce is also great brushed on shrimp while they are on the grill. See photograph, page 75.

2 dozen fresh oysters, in the shell

CHIPOTLE-LIME BUTTER
¼ pound unsalted butter, at room temperature
1 tablespoon chipotle chiles in adobo sauce, such as
*   Embasa brand in 4-ounce cans*
Juice and zest of 1 lime
Pinch of salt
3 slices lime, as garnish

Scrub the oyster shells under cold running water, then refrigerate. Place the butter, chiles, lime juice and zest, and salt in a food processor. Pulse the machine and process until completely smooth. If made more than 2 hours before cooking, refrigerate the butter mixture. *The recipe can be completed to this point up to 4 hours before cooking.*

If the butter is chilled, bring it to room temperature. Preheat a gas barbecue or indoor grill to medium (350°) or, if using charcoal or wood, prepare a fire and let it burn until the coals or wood are ash-covered. Brush the grill with oil. When the coals are still glowing red, place the oysters "boat"-side down on the grill and cook until they open, 3 to 6 minutes. As the oysters open, remove them using tongs. Separate the shells, being careful to keep the oyster juice in the "boat"-shaped half of the shell. The oysters will still be attached to the flat shell. Cut off the oysters and transfer the oysters to the shells holding the moisture. Transfer to a serving platter, and top each oyster with a small dollop of butter. Garnish with lime and serve immediately.

Pork Baby Back Ribs with Spicy Peanut Butter Slather

SERVES 6 TO 12

Few smells are as welcoming as that of ribs slow roasting in the oven. You'll find that dinner guests move without invitation towards the cooking ribs, and usually won't leave them unattended until just bones remain. You can keep cooked ribs warm for up to 1 hour if sealed inside a paper grocery bag, but don't cut them into individual ribs until just before serving, or they will lose much of their juiciness. See photograph, page 71.

1 side baby back ribs or your favorite ribs
Spicy Peanut Butter Marinade (page 73) or one of
*   the other marinades*

Loosen the tough, white membrane found on the underside of the ribs and, gripping it with a paper towel, pull it off. Rub the marinade over the ribs, refrigerate, and let them marinate at least 15 minutes. For more intense flavor, marinate longer. *The recipe can be completed to this point up to 8 hours before cooking.*

Preheat the oven to 325°. Place the ribs, meaty side up, on a wire rack. Set in a baking pan and roast until the meat begins to shrink from the ends of the bone, about 1 hour. (During roasting, do not turn the ribs over.) To serve, cut into individual ribs. Transfer to a heated serving platter and serve at once.

Chinese Chicken Wings

SERVES 6 TO 12

The group of chicken wing fanatics continues to grow. Always marinate chicken wings for at least 24 hours so the flavors permeate the meat.

4 pounds chicken wings (about 16 to 20)
Chinese Marinade (page 72) or one of the other marinades
1 tablespoon white sesame seeds, toasted

Cut off and discard the wing tips. In a large container, toss the wings with the marinade until well coated. Let the wings marinate, stirring 2 or 3 times, for 24 hours.

Preheat the oven to 375°. Line a shallow baking pan with foil. Add a rack sprayed with oil. Place the wings, smooth skin down, on the rack and roast 30 minutes. Brush the wings with marinade, turn them over, brush on more marinade, and roast another 30 minutes. Remove the wings from the oven. Using poultry shears or a knife, cut the wings in half through the joint. Serve at once. Or return the wings to the wire rack. Within 2 hours, reheat the wings in a 325° oven for 15 minutes. Sprinkle with the toasted sesame seeds. Transfer to a heated serving platter and serve at once.

From top: Pork Baby Back Ribs with
Spicy Peanut Butter Slather (page 69),
Chinese Chicken Wings

Beef Tenderloin in Our Favorite Barbecue Sauce

SERVES 12 TO 20

Barbecued, chilled, and thinly sliced beef tenderloin makes a great appetizer for both small and large parties. Simply place it on crackers and top it with a dip (pages 16–22). Or, for larger parties, serve the meat accompanied by thinly sliced baguette, mustard, chutney, and chopped herbs, and have everyone assemble their own little towers.

Our Favorite Barbecue Sauce (this page)
3 pounds beef tenderloin, trimmed of all silver skin and fat
Crackers or baguette slices, as accompaniment
Mustard, chutney, or dip (pages 16–22), as accompaniment

Rub the sauce over the beef, refrigerate, and let it marinate for 2 hours.

If grilling, preheat a gas barbecue or indoor grill to medium (350°) or, if using charcoal or wood, prepare a fire and let it burn until the coals or wood are ash-covered. Brush the grill with oil. If cooking in the oven, preheat to 500°. Place the tenderloin on the grill or on a wire rack elevated on a roasting pan in the oven. Barbecue or roast the tenderloin, brushing occasionally with additional marinade, until the internal temperature reaches 120° on an instant-read meat thermometer, about 20 minutes. Let cool, and then refrigerate until chilled, about 3 hours. Slice the meat across the grain into very thin slices. *The tenderloin can be prepared, covered with plastic wrap, and refrigerated up to 24 hours before serving.* Serve chilled, with crackers, baguette slices, mustard, chutney, and/or dip as accompaniments.

Marinades for Grilled or Oven-Roasted Appetizers

The following marinades are easy to prepare. Simply combine all of the ingredients for the marinade in a nonreactive bowl and stir well. Except for Mustard-Rosemary Marinade, which should be used the day it is made, all the other marinades can be made up to a week in advance if kept refrigerated. All these marinades have complex flavors. Experiment by brushing them on any meats, seafood, or vegetables that are going to be placed on skewers and grilled or broiled.

Our Favorite Barbecue Sauce

(for all seafood and meats)

MAKES 2 CUPS

1/2 cup hoisin sauce
1/3 cup plum sauce
1/4 cup oyster sauce
1/4 cup dry sherry
2 tablespoons white or red wine vinegar
2 tablespoons flavorless cooking oil
1 tablespoon Asian chile sauce
2 tablespoons finely minced ginger
5 cloves garlic, finely minced

Chinese Marinade

(for all seafood and meats)

MAKES 4 CUPS

1 cup hoisin sauce
3/4 cup plum sauce
1/2 cup thin or low-sodium soy sauce
1/3 cup white or red wine vinegar
1/4 cup dry sherry
1/4 cup honey
1/2 cup minced green onion
6 cloves garlic, finely minced
2 tablespoons finely minced ginger
1/4 cup white sesame seeds, toasted

Chipotle-Coriander Marinade

(for all meats)

MAKES 2 1/2 CUPS

1/4 cup chipotle chiles in adobo sauce, minced
   (both chiles and sauce)
1 cup ketchup
6 tablespoons brown sugar
1/4 cup molasses
1/4 cup thin, low-sodium, or dark soy sauce
1/4 cup cider vinegar
1 tablespoon grated orange zest
1 tablespoon ground coriander
8 cloves garlic, minced
2 shallots, peeled and minced

Spicy Peanut Butter Marinade

(for all meats)

MAKES 2 1/2 CUPS

1/2 cup chunky peanut butter
1/2 cup dry sherry
1/4 cup thin or low-sodium soy sauce
1/4 cup white or red wine vinegar
1/4 cup honey
2 tablespoons dark sesame oil
2 tablespoons Asian chile sauce
6 cloves garlic, finely minced
1/4 cup finely minced ginger
1/4 cup minced fresh cilantro sprigs

Mustard-Rosemary Marinade

(for all seafood and meats)

MAKES 1 3/4 CUPS

2 tablespoons minced tender rosemary leaves
4 cloves garlic, finely minced
1/3 cup Dijon mustard
1/3 cup dry white wine
1/3 cup freshly squeezed lemon juice
1/4 cup oyster sauce
1/4 cup honey
2 teaspoons hot sauce

Spicy Asian Marinade

(for all seafood and poultry)

MAKES 1 3/4 CUPS

2 tablespoons finely minced ginger
1/4 cup minced green onion
2 tablespoons chopped fresh cilantro sprigs
1 tablespoon finely minced lime zest
1/4 cup freshly squeezed lime juice
1/4 cup hoisin sauce
1/4 cup white or red wine vinegar
1/4 cup honey
2 tablespoons thin or low-sodium soy sauce
2 teaspoons hot sauce
2 tablespoons flavorless cooking oil

Salmon Satay

SERVES 4 TO 10

Skewered meats and seafood take little time to prepare, cook in minutes, offer an endless range of variations, and are easy to eat. We prefer using bamboo skewers rather than metal skewers, which have a metallic taste and invariably result in burned hands and lips. In addition to salmon, try these other meats and seafoods on skewers: firm-fleshed fish such as swordfish, shark, and tuna; fresh bay scallops or shrimp; beef tenderloin; and chicken thigh meat.

1 pound fresh salmon fillet, skinned and pin bones removed by the market
Mustard-Rosemary Marinade (page 73) or one of the other marinades

Cut the salmon into strips about ¼ inch by 1 inch by 4 inches. Twisting one bamboo skewer, run it lengthwise into each piece of fish, so that the tips are barely visible. Gently rub the marinade over the salmon. Pour the excess marinade into a small, nonreactive bowl or Pyrex measuring cup and stand the skewers of salmon upright (salmon end down) in the marinade. Refrigerate. *The recipe can be completed to this point up to 8 hours before cooking.*

Preheat a gas barbecue or indoor grill to medium (350°) or, if using charcoal or wood, prepare a fire and let it burn until the coals or wood are ash-covered. Lay a doubled strip of foil, 4 inches wide, along the section of the grill that is the most evenly heated. Brush the grill with oil. Lay the salmon on the grill so the exposed skewers are protected from the heat by the foil. Grill the salmon about 1 minute on each side, or until it has lost its raw outside color and is still slightly undercooked in the center. Or, to broil the salmon, preheat the oven to 500°. Place the salmon skewers on a wire rack set in a shallow roasting pan and cover the exposed bamboo ends with a strip of foil. Broil the salmon about 1 minute on each side. Remove foil. Transfer to a heated platter and serve at once.

From left: Salmon Satay, Barbecued Oysters with Chipotle-Lime Butter (page 69)

Meatball Appetizers East and West

Meatballs are a popular appetizer, for both cook and guest. The filling takes just minutes to combine, and only about 10 minutes to roll into little balls. They can be stored in the refrigerator for up to 12 hours, then it's simply a matter of popping them under the broiler or on the barbecue and serving them piping hot to eager throngs. Don't be tempted to freeze raw or cooked meatballs. No matter how carefully they are defrosted, the meat will have lost all its juiciness.

Spicy Southwest Meatballs with Sharp Cheddar and Pine Nuts

SERVES 6 TO 12

The quality of ground chicken and turkey varies drastically. Be sure to ask your butcher if the market grinds the chicken and turkey daily. If the meat is preground at some distant location, substitute ground lamb, veal, or pork.

$^1/_4$ cup pine nuts
$^3/_4$ pound freshly ground chicken or turkey
$^3/_4$ cup grated sharp Cheddar cheese
2 tablespoons minced fresh cilantro sprigs
2 cloves garlic, finely minced
1 teaspoon crushed red pepper flakes
$^1/_4$ teaspoon salt
$^1/_2$ cup unseasoned bread crumbs

Preheat the oven to 325°. Spread the pine nuts on a baking sheet and toast in the oven until golden, about 8 minutes.

In a bowl, combine the ground chicken, cheese, pine nuts, cilantro, garlic, pepper flakes, and salt. Using your hands, mix well. Lightly oil your hands. Form the meat into about 24 $^1/_2$-inch-diameter meatballs by rolling the meat between your palms. Roll the meatballs in the bread crumbs. Place on a baking sheet lined with foil and refrigerate. *The recipe can be completed to this point up to 12 hours before cooking.*

Preheat the oven to 400°, then turn the oven setting to broil. Place the baking sheet of meatballs 4 inches below the broiler. Broil for 3 minutes (do not turn meatballs during cooking). Transfer to a serving platter and serve at once with toothpicks.

Mediterranean Meatballs with Olives and Feta

SERVES 6 TO 12

There are many ways to vary the flavor of these meatballs. Add one or any combination of the following: 1 tablespoon minced basil, ¼ cup grated Parmesan, and 2 tablespoons chopped roasted hazelnuts.

³/₄ pound ground veal
¼ pound imported Greek feta cheese, crumbled
¼ cup chopped pitted imported black olives, such as kalamata
2 tablespoons minced bottled roasted red peppers
2 cloves garlic, finely minced
1 teaspoon grated lemon zest
½ teaspoon crushed red pepper flakes
½ cup unseasoned bread crumbs

In a bowl, combine the veal, feta, olives, red pepper, garlic, lemon zest, and pepper flakes. Using your hands, mix well. Lightly oil your hands. Form the meat into about 24 ½-inch-diameter meatballs by rolling the meat between your palms. Roll the meatballs in the bread crumbs. Place on a baking sheet lined with foil and refrigerate. *The recipe can be completed to this point up to 8 hours before cooking.*

Preheat the oven to 400°, then turn the oven setting to broil. Place the baking sheet of meatballs 4 inches below the broiler. Broil 3 minutes (do not turn the meatballs during cooking). Transfer to a serving plate and serve at once with toothpicks.

Caribbean Meatballs on Skewers

SERVES 6 TO 12

The combination of herbs, ginger, chile, and nutmeg gives these meatballs an alluring flavor. If you barbecue the meatballs, be sure the grill is well oiled so the meatballs don't stick to the cooking grate. See photograph, pages 78–79.

³/₄ pound ground pork, veal, or lamb
2 tablespoons chopped fresh cilantro sprigs
2 tablespoons chopped fresh mint
2 tablespoons finely minced ginger
2 teaspoons hot sauce
1 tablespoon oyster sauce or thin or low-sodium soy sauce
³/₄ teaspoon freshly grated nutmeg
2 tablespoons flavorless cooking oil
½ cup unseasoned bread crumbs
12 bamboo skewers
1 cup Sweet-and-Sour Apricot Dip (page 17)

In a bowl, combine the pork, cilantro, mint, ginger, hot sauce, oyster sauce, and nutmeg. Using your hands, mix well. Lightly oil your hands. Form the meat into about 24 ½-inch-diameter meatballs by rolling the meat between your palms. Roll the meatballs in the bread crumbs. Place 2 meatballs on a bamboo skewer, repeat with remaining meatballs, and refrigerate. Prepare the dipping sauce. *The recipe can be completed to this point up to 12 hours before grilling.*

Preheat a gas barbecue or indoor grill to medium (350°) or, if using charcoal or wood, prepare a fire and let it burn until the coals or wood are ash-covered. Brush the meatballs with the Sweet-and-Sour Apricot Dip. When the grill is hot, brush it with oil. Place a double layer of aluminum foil across the bottom third of the grill. Place the meatballs on the grill so the exposed skewers are protected from the heat by the foil. Grill the meatballs until cooked through, about 2 minutes. Turn them over halfway through the cooking. Serve at once.

Spicy Thai Meatballs Wrapped with Lettuce

SERVES 6 TO 12

Thai cooks would use ground pork, but we prefer the more intense flavor of ground lamb. Each person can wrap a meatball in lettuce and dip the package into a sauce. (And repeat again and again.)

³/₄ pound ground lamb
1 whole green onion, finely minced
2 tablespoons minced fresh cilantro sprigs
2 cloves garlic, finely minced
¹/₂ teaspoon finely minced orange zest
2 tablespoons thin or low-sodium soy sauce
2 teaspoons Asian chile sauce
2 tablespoons flavorless cooking oil
¹/₂ cup unseasoned bread crumbs
1 head Bibb lettuce
24 fresh mint leaves, chilled
Thai Tomato Salsa (page 17)

In a bowl, combine the lamb, green onion, cilantro, garlic, orange zest, soy, and chile sauce. Using your hands, mix thoroughly. Lightly oil your hands. Form the meat into about 24 ¹/₂-inch-diameter meatballs by rolling it between your palms. Roll the meatballs in the bread crumbs, transfer to a baking sheet lined with foil, and refrigerate.

Separate the lettuce into 24 small cups. Refrigerate the lettuce and mint leaves. Prepare the dipping sauce. *The recipe can be completed to this point up to 12 hours before cooking.*

Preheat the oven to 400°, then turn the oven setting to broil. Place the baking sheet of meatballs 4 inches below the broiler. Broil 3 minutes (do not turn the meatballs over during cooking). Remove the meatballs from the oven. Place the lettuce cups on a serving platter. Add a mint leaf and a meatball to each lettuce cup. Place 1 teaspoon dipping sauce on the meatballs. Serve at once.

Spicy Thai Meatballs Wrapped with Lettuce and Caribbean Meatballs on Skewers (page 77) with (left) Sweet-and-Sour Apricot Dip (page 17) and (right) Basil Ponzu Sauce (page 47)

Flaky Pastry Packages

*P*hyllo dough and puff pastry are available frozen at all supermarkets. Easy to work with, they can be used to create a never-ending array of elegant, flavorful appetizers. The fillings for these appetizers take only minutes to make, but the folding takes time. Fortunately, all these appetizers can be stored for up to 3 months in the freezer, so the only last-minute work is transferring them from freezer to oven.

Crisp Pastry Sticks

MAKES 24

These are spicy, delicious nibbles that come together in a snap. The dough is quickly made in a food processor, then rolled out, cut into strips, and baked in the oven. See photograph, page 82.

2 cloves garlic, peeled
1 small shallot, peeled
1 cup unbleached white flour, plus extra to roll out the dough
1 teaspoon ground coriander
1 teaspoon salt
1/2 teaspoon ground cumin
1/2 teaspoon sugar
1/2 teaspoon cayenne pepper
8 tablespoons chilled butter, cut into 10 pieces
2 tablespoons ice water
1 egg white, lightly beaten
1/3 cup finely grated Parmesan cheese

*I*n a food processor, mince the garlic and shallot. Add 1 cup of the flour, the coriander, salt, cumin, sugar, cayenne, and butter. Pulse until the mixture resembles coarse meal or has formed into little balls. If the dough resembles coarse meal, with the machine running, add enough water (1 to 2 tablespoons) to make the dough form little balls. Remove the dough from the food processor and, using your hands, form it into a ball. Cover with plastic wrap and refrigerate for 15 minutes.

On a floured surface, roll the dough out into a sheet 1/8-inch thick. Brush with the egg white, sprinkle with the Parmesan cheese, and cut into 3/4-inch-wide strips. Transfer the strips onto a baking sheet lined with parchment paper. Refrigerate for 15 minutes.

Preheat the oven to 350°. Bake the strips until golden and crisp, 20 to 25 minutes. Serve warm from the oven, or cool on a wire rack and store layered between sheets of parchment or wax paper in an airtight container at room temperature. *The pastry can be made up to 2 days before serving.*

Spicy Puff Pastry Cheese Straws

MAKES 40 TO 48

Use any aged cheese (Parmesan, sharp Cheddar, dry Monterey jack, Asiago) hard enough to be grated to a fine powder. Just cut the cheese into cubes and, using a food processor fitted with a standard blade, process until finely powdered. See photograph, page 82.

¹/₄ cup all-purpose flour
1 sheet puff pastry (half of a 17¹/₄-ounce box), at room
   temperature
1¹/₂ cups finely grated Parmesan cheese
1 teaspoon crushed red pepper flakes
¹/₄ cup chopped fresh cilantro sprigs
1 egg white, lightly beaten
3 tablespoons white sesame seeds

On a lightly floured surface, roll the puff pastry out into a 12 by 18-inch rectangle. Place the pastry so the long side is facing you. Cover the right half of the dough with ¹/₃ of the cheese. Fold the left half over. Press lightly and roll out into a 12 by 18-inch rectangle. Cover the right half of dough with ¹/₃ of the cheese. Fold the left half over. Press and lightly roll out into a 12 by 18-inch rectangle.

Cover the right half of the dough with the remaining cheese, and sprinkle on the red pepper flakes and cilantro. Fold the left half over. Roll the dough into a 12 by 12-inch rectangle. Cut in half, brush with egg white, and sprinkle with sesame seeds.

Using a knife or cutting wheel, cut the pastry into ¹/₂ by 6-inch strips. Twist each strip and transfer to baking sheets lined with parchment paper. Preheat the oven to 425°. Bake the cheese straws until golden, about 8 minutes. Serve warm from the oven, or cool on a wire rack and store in an airtight container at room temperature. *The cheese straws can be made up to 2 days before serving.* Serve at room temperature or warmed in a 350° oven for 3 minutes.

Phyllo Coins Filled with Spicy Orange Lamb

SERVES 6 TO 10

Unlike the Beggar's Purses (page 83), these coins cannot be frozen. If you cook these frozen, the meat filling will still be raw when the phyllo is done. And if you freeze and defrost the appetizer before baking, the phyllo becomes soggy. However, you can assemble and then refrigerate these 8 hours before baking.

¹/₄ pound unsalted butter
3 sheets phyllo dough

MEAT FILLING
¹/₂ pound ground lamb or veal
2 green onions, finely minced
¹/₄ cup chopped fresh cilantro sprigs
1 tablespoon finely minced ginger
1 teaspoon grated orange zest
3 cloves garlic, finely minced
1 tablespoon oyster sauce
2 teaspoons Asian chile sauce or hot sauce
1 teaspoon sugar

In a small saucepan over low heat, melt the butter. Lift off any butter solids that float to the surface. In a bowl, combine all of the ingredients for the meat filling. Using your hands, mix thoroughly.

Working on a flat surface, brush a sheet of the phyllo dough with butter. Top with another sheet of phyllo, brush with butter, and repeat with the remaining sheet of phyllo. Spoon the meat filling along the longest edge of the phyllo. Roll the phyllo into a cylinder, brushing a little butter along the edge to seal the cylinder. Transfer, edge side down, onto a baking sheet lined with parchment paper.

Brush the sides and the top of the cylinder with butter. Using a serrated knife, cut the cylinder into 16 1-inch-thick "coins," but do not separate them. Cover loosely with plastic wrap and refrigerate until ready to bake. *The recipe can be completed to this point up to 8 hours before baking.*

To serve, preheat the oven to 400°. Bake the phyllo coins until golden, about 15 minutes. Transfer to a serving plate and serve at once.

Beggar's Purses with Warm Goat Cheese

SERVES 6 TO 12

This simple but delicious appetizer is the creation of Cakebread Winery chef Brian Streeter. In terms of do-ahead ideas, this appetizer is best if frozen and then baked frozen. By the time the phyllo turns golden brown, the goat cheese filling will be perfectly warm.

4 ounces unsalted butter
3 (12 by 17½-inch) sheets phyllo dough

GOAT CHEESE-CHIVE FILLING
4 ounces soft goat cheese
1 teaspoon chopped chives
1 teaspoon grated lemon zest

In a small saucepan over low heat, melt the butter. Lift off any butter solids that float to the surface. In a bowl, mix together the goat cheese, chives, and lemon zest.

Working on a flat surface, brush a sheet of the phyllo dough with butter. Top with another sheet of phyllo, and brush with butter. Add the last sheet of phyllo and brush with butter. These sheets will become your wrapping. Cut the phyllo into 20 squares measuring 3 by 3 inches. Place 2 teaspoons of the filling in the center of each square. Pull all the edges up to form a little purse and place on a baking sheet lined with parchment paper. Refrigerate up to 4 hours or freeze. *The beggar's purses can be completed to this point up to 2 weeks before cooking.*

To serve, preheat the oven to 400°. Place the frozen or refrigerated beggar's purses in the oven and bake until golden, about 8 minutes if fresh and about 15 minutes if frozen. Serve warm.

Beggar's Purses with Warm Goat Cheese with
(left) Crisp Pastry Sticks (page 80) and (right)
Spicy Puff Pastry Cheese Straws (page 81)

The following three fillings can be substituted for the Goat Cheese–Chive Filling in the previous recipe. Just fold, freeze, and bake the beggar's purses as described on the left.

Cranberry and Orange Zest Filling

4 ounces soft goat cheese
¼ cup dried cranberries
1 teaspoon grated orange zest
1 teaspoon chopped fresh chives

In a bowl, combine all of the ingredients and mix well.

Ginger, Chile, and Goat Cheese Filling

2 tablespoons pine nuts
4 ounces soft goat cheese
1 tablespoon finely minced ginger
1 tablespoon chopped fresh cilantro sprigs
½ teaspoon Asian chile sauce

Preheat the oven to 325°. Spread the pine nuts on a baking sheet and toast until golden, about 8 minutes. In a bowl, combine all of the ingredients and mix well.

Gorgonzola, Walnut, and Roasted Red Pepper Filling

½ cup walnuts
4 ounces Gorgonzola or other blue cheese
¼ cup chopped bottled roasted red peppers

Preheat the oven to 325°. Spread the walnuts on a baking sheet and toast until golden brown, about 15 minutes. Let cool and coarsely chop. Place 2 teaspoons of blue cheese in the phyllo square. Add 1 to 3 pieces of walnuts and a piece of red pepper. Shape into purses.

Phyllo Triangles with Secret Treasures

SERVES 6 TO 12

Little phyllo triangles, golden, hot, and hiding a savory filling, make great appetizers. The crisp, buttery pastry contrasts deliciously with any of the four filling recipes that follow. The key is to fold the phyllo into bite-size triangles. It is terribly messy biting into a too-large triangle, and the crisp phyllo pieces will leave a trail of evidence everywhere!

4 ounces unsalted butter
2 sheets phyllo dough
Spicy Shrimp, Curried Meat, Goat Cheese-Peppercorn,
*   or Mushroom-Cheese Filling*

*I*n a small saucepan over low heat, melt the butter. Lift off any butter solids that float on the surface. Working on a flat surface, brush a sheet of the phyllo dough with butter. Top with another sheet of phyllo. Cut the sheet lengthwise into 8 equal strips, then cut the strips in half at the middle. Place 2 teaspoons of filling at the end of a strip. Beginning at the filling end of the strip, fold back and forth into a triangle shape until all the phyllo strip is used. Repeat with the remaining strips. Place on a baking sheet lined with cooking parchment paper. Brush the tops with butter, cover with plastic wrap, and refrigerate or freeze until ready to bake. *The triangles can be refrigerated for 1 day or frozen for up to 2 weeks before baking.*

To serve, preheat the oven to 400°. Do not thaw the triangles if frozen. Bake until golden, about 10 minutes if refrigerated or 15 minutes if frozen. Serve at once.

Spicy Shrimp Filling

1 whole green onion
1/2 pound raw medium shrimp, shelled and deveined
1 tablespoon finely minced ginger
1 tablespoon oyster sauce
1 teaspoon Asian chile sauce or hot sauce

*I*n a food processor, separately mince the green onion and shrimp. In a bowl, combine the green onion, shrimp, ginger, oyster sauce, and chile sauce. Using your hands, mix thoroughly.

Curried Meat Filling

1/2 pound ground lamb, pork, or veal
2 tablespoons minced green onion
2 tablespoons chopped fresh cilantro
1 tablespoon finely minced ginger
1 clove garlic, minced
1 tablespoon oyster sauce or thin or low-sodium soy sauce
2 teaspoons curry powder
1 teaspoon Asian chile sauce or hot sauce

*I*n a bowl, combine all of the ingredients. Using your hands, mix thoroughly.

Goat Cheese-Peppercorn Filling

1 tablespoon tricolored peppercorn mix
1 teaspoon grated orange zest
2 tablespoons minced fresh mint
6 ounces soft goat cheese
1/4 cup freshly grated Parmesan cheese
1/4 cup dried cranberries, chopped

*I*n an ungreased skillet over medium heat, toast the peppercorns until they just begin to smoke. Let cool slightly, then coarsely grind in an electric spice grinder or with a mortar and pestle. In a bowl, combine the ground pepper and all of the remaining ingredients. Using your hands, mix thoroughly.

Mushroom-Cheese Filling

1/2 pound fresh shiitake mushrooms
2 tablespoons unsalted butter
2 cloves garlic, minced
1 whole green onion, minced
1/4 cup chopped fresh parsley
6 ounces soft goat cheese or ricotta cheese
1/2 teaspoon freshly ground black pepper
1/4 teaspoon salt

*D*iscard the mushroom stems. Cut the caps in half, then cut crosswise into 1/4-inch slices. Place a 12-inch sauté pan over medium heat. Add the butter, and when it just begins to brown, add the mushrooms and garlic. Sauté until the mushrooms become completely wilted, about 4 minutes. Transfer to a bowl and let cool to room temperature. Add all of the remaining ingredients and, using your hands, mix thoroughly.

New Ideas for Pizzas

Pizzas cut into thin wedges or bite-size squares make appetizers that will please everybody. Avoid the temptation to crown the pizza with so many toppings that it's transformed from an appetizer to an entrée. Instead, use only a few flavorful ingredients.

For the fastest pizza appetizers, opt for a 10-inch flour tortilla (very good as a pizza dough substitute) or for a store-bought thin crust such as Boboli (our least favorite choice). Time permitting, make your own dough, or buy it from an Italian restaurant or pizza parlor. You can even precook the crust at 500° until it just loses its raw outside color, about 3 minutes. When the guests arrive, just add the toppings and bake.

Pizza Dough

MAKES ONE 10- TO 12-INCH PIZZA CRUST

Here is a very easy pizza dough that can be made ahead and refrigerated until you are ready to use it. For the best-tasting results, use a wooden pizza peel to transfer the pizza dough in and out of the oven, and cook the pizza on a large, thick pizza stone. Only a pizza stone, preheated in a very hot oven, will vaporize the moisture on the underside of the dough and create a crisp crust.

2 cups unbleached white flour
$^3/_4$ cup warm water
2 teaspoons dry yeast
1 tablespoon sugar
1 tablespoon extra virgin olive oil
$1^1/_2$ teaspoons salt

Place flour in the food processor. In a bowl, combine the water, yeast, and sugar. When the yeast bubbles, add the olive oil and the salt. With the food processor on, add the water mixture to the flour. When it forms a ball, turn onto a floured surface and knead until smooth and no longer sticky, about 5 minutes. Transfer to a bowl that has been lightly coated with olive oil; rotate the dough so that it is lightly coated in oil, cover, and let rise until it doubles in size, 1 to 2 hours. If making the dough more than 3 hours ahead, let the dough rise in the refrigerator. *The recipe can be completed to this point up to 12 hours before baking.*

Spicy Three-Cheese Pizza with Herbs

SERVES 6 TO 12

Given the fantastic array of domestic and imported cheeses now available, why limit pizza toppings to mozzarella and grated Parmesan cheese? Don't be afraid to experiment. Ask the person behind the cheese counter to recommend a couple of cheeses for pizza. Buy at least one aged cheese and one cheese that melts easily. Some of the cheeses we have especially enjoyed on pizzas include imported aged Provolone, imported aged or young Asiago, Bel Paese, Taleggio, mascarpone, Gruyère, Teleme, and aged or young goat cheese.

2 tablespoons extra virgin olive oil
2 cloves garlic, finely minced
1½ ounces aged Provolone cheese (½ cup shredded)
1½ ounces aged or young Asiago or Parmesan cheese
    (½ cup shredded)
1½ ounces Bel Paese, Taleggio, or mozzarella cheese
    (½ cup shredded)
3 tablespoons pine nuts
Fresh pizza dough (homemade or purchased from a
    pizza parlor), 1 (10-inch) tortilla, or 1 thin-crust
    storebought pizza dough
¼ cup cornmeal
¼ cup chopped fresh basil or cilantro

In a small bowl, combine the olive oil and garlic. Shred the cheese; then refrigerate. Preheat the oven to 325°. Spread the pine nuts on a baking sheet and toast until golden, about 8 minutes. *The recipe can be completed to this point up to 8 hours before cooking.*

For fresh pizza dough: Place a pizza stone in the oven and preheat at 500° for 1 hour. Roll the pizza dough out into a 10-inch circle on a lightly floured surface. Brush the olive oil and garlic over the top of the crust. Sprinkle a pizza paddle with cornmeal. Gently lay the dough on top of the paddle and sprinkle on the cheeses. Slide the pizza onto the preheated pizza stone in the oven. Bake until the crust is golden, about 12 minutes. Remove from the oven.

For storebought pizza dough and tortillas: Place the pizza stone in the oven and preheat at 500° for 1 hour. If you have a gas stovetop, then lightly char the tortilla on both sides. Add the toppings. Slide the pizza onto the pizza stone, 4 inches below the broiler heat. When the cheese melts, about 4 minutes, remove from the oven.

Sprinkle the hot pizza with the basil or cilantro and pine nuts. Cut into wedges or bite-size squares, and serve at once.

Three Pizza Toppings

Here are three unique pizza toppings to use on fresh pizza dough, a thin-crust storebought pizza dough, or a 10-inch flour tortilla. Follow the baking instructions outlined for the Spicy Three-Cheese Pizza with Herbs (left).

Goat Cheese and Roasted Red Pepper Topping

SERVES 6 TO 1

This easy pizza topping calls for bottled roasted red peppers, which you can find in the pickle and relish section of supermarkets. Or substitute fresh red bell peppers and roast them as described on page 13.

2 tablespoons extra virgin olive oil
3 cloves garlic, finely minced
½ teaspoon crushed red pepper flakes
1 cup bottled roasted red peppers, drained
1½ ounces aged Gouda cheese (½ cup shredded)
1½ ounces soft goat cheese (½ cup crumbled)
¼ cup chopped fresh basil or cilantro sprigs

In a small bowl, combine the olive oil, garlic, and pepper flakes. Cut the red peppers into bite-size pieces and set aside. Shred the Gouda and crumble the goat cheese; refrigerate. *The recipe can be competed to this point up to 8 hours before cooking.*

Brush the olive oil over the top of the crust. Place all of the toppings except the herbs on the crust. Bake according to the directions for the Spicy Three-Cheese Pizza with Herbs (left). Remove the pizza from the oven and sprinkle on the chopped basil or cilantro. Cut the pizza into wedges or bite-size squares and serve at once.

Wild Mushroom Topping

SERVES 6 TO 12

Any mix of firm fresh mushrooms works well in this recipe, but soft-textured mushrooms like enoki or oyster will become mushy.

¹/₄ cup unsalted butter
2 cloves garlic, finely minced
¹/₂ pound fresh portobello mushrooms, thinly sliced
¹/₄ pound fresh shiitake mushrooms, thinly sliced
¹/₄ pound fresh chanterelle mushrooms, thinly sliced
1 tablespoon oyster sauce or thin or low-sodium soy sauce
2 ounces Gruyère cheese (³/₄ cup shredded)
2 tablespoons extra virgin olive oil
3 tablespoons chopped fresh basil
Freshly ground black pepper

Place a 12-inch sauté pan over medium heat. Add the butter and garlic. When the butter begins to brown, add the mushrooms. Stir and toss the mushrooms until they wilt, about 5 minutes. Add the oyster sauce or soy sauce and continue cooking the mushrooms until they are completely wilted and all the moisture has evaporated. Transfer the mushrooms to a plate, let cool, cover with plastic wrap, and refrigerate. Shred the cheese and set aside. *The recipe can be completed to this point up to 8 hours before cooking.*

Brush the olive oil over the top of the crust. Place all of the toppings except the basil and black pepper on the crust. Bake according to the directions for the Spicy Three-Cheese Pizza with Herbs (page 87). Remove the pizza from the oven and sprinkle with the basil and pepper. Cut the pizza into wedges or bite-size squares and serve at once.

Thai Shrimp Pizza Topping

SERVES 6 TO 12

Raw shrimp are cut in half lengthwise and then sprinkled over the crust with the other toppings. They cook perfectly by the time the cheese bubbles.

¹/₃ cup canned tomato sauce
1 clove garlic, finely minced
2 teaspoons Asian chile sauce or hot sauce
¹/₃ pound raw medium shrimp, shelled and deveined
1¹/₂ ounces Gruyère cheese (¹/₂ cup shredded)
1¹/₂ ounces aged or fresh goat cheese
* (¹/₂ cup grated or crumbled)*
¹/₄ cup chopped fresh cilantro
1 teaspoon grated lime zest

In a bowl, combine the tomato sauce, garlic, and chile sauce and mix well. Split the shrimp in half lengthwise and refrigerate. Shred or crumble the cheese, and refrigerate. *The recipe can be completed to this point up to 8 hours before cooking.*

Place all of the toppings except the cilantro and lime zest on the crust. Bake according to the directions for the Spicy Three-Cheese Pizza with Herbs (page 87). Remove the pizza from the oven and sprinkle on the cilantro and lime zest. Cut the pizza into wedges or bite-size squares and serve at once.

Pizzas with (left) Thai Shrimp Pizza Topping
and (right) Wild Mushroom Topping

Quick Tex-Mex Appetizers

These nachos and quesadillas are power-packed appetizers, rich in flavor, texture, and color. But they are power packed in calories, too! Serve a variety of these at an appetizer party where little nibbles are the main event. However, if appetizers precede dinner, limit yourself to one choice and accompany it with chilled asparagus or chilled cooked shrimp.

Power Nachos

SERVES 4 TO 8

Nachos must have lots of cheese and be cooked on a heat-proof dish that doubles as the serving plate. Even dinner guests planning a long vacation at the local diet center will plow through these. See photograph, page 93.

$1/_2$ cup taco sauce, such as La Victoria Red Taco Sauce
2 teaspoons hot sauce, or more to taste
$1/_4$ cup pecans
4 cups lightly salted tortilla chips
$1^1/_2$ cups grated Monterey jack or sharp Cheddar cheese
$1/_2$ cup minced red onion
$1/_4$ cup chopped fresh cilantro

Preheat the oven to 325°. In a small bowl, combine the taco sauce and hot sauce. Spread the pecans on a baking sheet and toast until golden brown, about 15 minutes. Let cool, then chop coarsely. *The recipe can be completed to this point up to 8 hours before cooking.*

Preheat the oven to 500°. Place the chips in a shallow heat-proof serving dish. Sprinkle them with half the cheese, drizzle on the taco sauce, and top with the onion and the rest of the cheese. Place in the oven and cook until the cheese melts, about 5 minutes. Sprinkle on the pecans and cilantro. Serve immediately.

Tex-Chinese Nachos

SERVES 4 TO 8

A little hoisin sauce and Asian chile sauce contribute a spicy, rich tasting flair to these nachos. To speed the serving of these, place the sour cream in a squeeze bottle so you can zigzag it across the top of the cooked nachos.

½ cup bottled spaghetti sauce
1 tablespoon hoisin sauce
1 tablespoon Asian chile sauce or hot sauce
2 cloves garlic
¼ cup sour cream
4 cups lightly salted tortilla chips
1½ cups sharp white or orange Cheddar cheese
¼ cup chopped fresh cilantro sprigs

*I*n a small bowl, combine the spaghetti sauce, hoisin sauce, chile sauce, and garlic and mix well. Place the sour cream in a plastic squeeze bottle. *The recipe can be completed to this point up to 8 hours before cooking.*

Preheat the oven to 500°. Place the chips in a shallow ovenproof serving dish. Sprinkle the chips with half the cheese, drizzle on the spaghetti sauce, and top with the remaining cheese. Place in the oven and cook until the cheese melts. Sprinkle on the cilantro. Zigzag the sour cream across the top. Serve immediately.

Quesadilla with Roasted Red Pepper, Pine Nuts, and Cheese

SERVES 6 TO 10

The secret to this recipe is to use the very best cheese. If you can't find aged Monterey Jack, substitute Provolone, Parmesan, or another aged hard-textured cheese.

2 tablespoons pine nuts
3 tablespoons taco sauce, such as La Victoria Red Taco Sauce
1 tablespoon hot sauce, or more to taste
2 (10-inch) flour tortillas
½ cup grated aged dry Monterey jack
⅓ cup chopped and drained bottled roasted red peppers
¼ cup chopped fresh cilantro sprigs
3 ounces soft goat cheese, crumbled
½ tablespoon unsalted butter

*P*reheat the oven to 325°. Spread the pine nuts on a baking sheet and bake in the oven until golden, about 8 minutes. Combine the taco sauce with the hot sauce. *The recipe can be completed to this point up to 8 hours before cooking.*

Place a tortilla on a flat surface. Sprinkle the tortilla with half the Monterey jack. Layer on the roasted red pepper, pine nuts, taco sauce mixture, cilantro, the rest of the jack cheese, and goat cheese. Cover with the second tortilla and press firmly. Set aside on a plate.

Place a 12-inch sauté pan over medium-high heat until hot. Add the butter. When the butter melts and begins to bubble, carefully transfer the quesadilla to the pan and place a small plate on top (the weight will help give it a nice texture). Cook until golden, 30 to 60 seconds. Remove the plate, turn the quesadilla, top with the plate, and cook another 30 to 60 seconds. The quesadilla should be golden on both sides. Cut the quesadilla into wedges. Transfer to a serving platter and serve at once. *The quesadilla can be cooked up to 2 hours before serving, refrigerated, and reheated in a 500° oven for 5 minutes.*

Quesadillas with Barbecued Meat and Brie

SERVES 4 TO 6

This is a very easy and utterly delicious appetizer. To save time, use your own barbecue sauce, and purchase the barbecued (or roasted) meat from a nearby market—it's especially good made with roast chicken or beef. Quesadillas taste best when cooked in a frying pan with a little butter, but they can also be cooked on the barbecue or baked in a 400° oven until heated through.

$^1/_4$ pound barbecued or roasted meat
$^1/_2$ papaya, not quite ripe
$^1/_4$ pound Brie cheese
4 (10-inch) flour tortillas
$^1/_4$ cup Our Favorite Barbecue Sauce (page 72)
     or bottled barbecue sauce
1 whole green onion, minced
$^1/_4$ cup chopped fresh cilantro sprigs
1 tablespoon unsalted butter

Cut the meat into very thin slices. Peel, seed, and cut the papaya into very thin slices. Cut the Brie into very thin pieces. *The recipe can be completed to this point up to 8 hours before cooking.*

Place a tortilla on a flat surface and spread the barbecue sauce evenly across the surface. Layer on half the meat, papaya, Brie, green onion, and cilantro. Cover with the second tortilla and press firmly. Set aside on a plate. Repeat for the second quesadilla.

Place a 12-inch sauté pan over medium-high heat until hot. Add half the butter. When the butter melts and begins to bubble, carefully transfer the quesadilla to the pan and place a small plate on top (the weight will help give it a nice texture). Cook until golden, 30 to 60 seconds. Remove the plate, turn the quesadilla, top with the plate, and cook another 30 to 60 seconds. The quesadilla should be golden on both sides. Repeat for second quesadilla. Cut the quesadillas into wedges. Transfer to a serving platter and serve at once. *The quesadillas can be cooked up to 2 hours before serving, refrigerated, and reheated in a 500° oven for 5 minutes.*

*From left: Quesadillas with Barbecued Meat
and Brie, Power Nachos (page 90)*

Quesadilla with Shrimp, Chiles, and Lime Zest

SERVES 6 TO 10

Unlike shrimp pizzas, where the shrimp are added raw to the pizza topping before baking, for quesadillas the shrimp must be cooked before they are sandwiched between the tortillas.

2 ounces medium cooked shrimp (boiled or barbecued)
1 ounce Parmesan cheese ($^1/_4$ cup grated)
$^1/_2$ cup shredded mozzarella cheese
2 (10-inch) flour tortillas
$^1/_4$ cup taco sauce, such as La Victoria Red Taco Sauce
1 jalapeño chile, seeds included, finely minced
1 tablespoon chopped fresh mint
1 tablespoon chopped fresh cilantro sprigs
$^1/_2$ teaspoon grated lime zest
$^1/_2$ tablespoon unsalted butter

Split the shrimp in half. Shred or grate the cheese; refrigerate. *The recipe can be completed to this point up to 8 hours before cooking.*

Place a tortilla on a flat surface. Layer on the Parmesan, shrimp, mozzarella, taco sauce, chile, herbs, and lime zest. Cover with the second tortilla and press firmly. Set aside on a plate.

Place a 12-inch sauté pan over medium-high heat until hot. Add the butter. When the butter melts and begins to bubble, carefully transfer the quesadilla to the pan and place a small plate on top (the weight will help give it a nice texture). Cook until golden, 30 to 60 seconds. Remove the plate, turn the quesadilla, top with the plate, and cook another 30 to 60 seconds. The quesadilla should be golden on both sides. Cut the quesadilla into wedges. Transfer to a serving platter and serve at once. *The quesadilla can be cooked up to 2 hours before serving, refrigerated, and reheated in a 500° oven for 5 minutes.*

Spicy Mexican Pizza

SERVES 6 TO 10

We couldn't resist adding this delicious and simple Mexican "pizza" to this chapter. If you can't get a fresh poblano chile, substitute a fresh Anaheim chile or a fresh red bell pepper.

2 fresh poblano or Anaheim chiles
2 tablespoons pine nuts
2 (10-inch) flour tortillas
1 tablespoon cornmeal
$^1/_4$ cup taco sauce, such as La Victoria Red Taco Sauce
2 jalapeño chiles, seeds included, minced
$^3/_4$ cup Monterey jack or Cheddar cheese
2 tablespoons chopped fresh cilantro

Roast the poblano chiles over a gas stove-top flame turned to high or under the broiler until lightly blackened on all sides. Seal in a zip-top bag for 15 minutes. Rub off the charred skin. Stem, seed, and cut the chiles into $^1/_4$-inch-wide long strips. Preheat the oven to 325°. Spread the pine nuts on a baking sheet and toast in the oven until golden, about 8 minutes. *The recipe can be completed to this point up to 8 hours before cooking.*

Preheat the oven to 500° (if you have a pizza stone, place in the oven before preheating the oven, then preheat the oven for 1 hour). If you have a gas stove top, lightly char the tortillas on both sides. Place the tortillas on a wooden pizza paddle lightly sprinkled with cornmeal. Spread the taco sauce evenly across the surface. Layer on the fresh jalapeño chiles and the cheese. Place the poblano chile strips on the pizza so they radiate outward from the center. Sprinkle with the pine nuts. Slide the pizzas onto the pizza stone, or place the pizzas on a baking sheet in the oven. Bake until the cheese bubbles, about 5 minutes. Remove from the oven and sprinkle with the cilantro. Cut into wedges and serve at once.

Out of the Wok in Seconds

When you think of appetizers, stir-fry might not be the first thing to come to mind. However, we love to serve stir-fries as starters. They have lots of flavor, the preparation can be completed hours in advance, and the last-minute cooking takes only seconds. Just before the guests arrive, place the wok or sauté pan over the lowest possible heat and assemble the ingredients next to the wok. Then when you are ready to serve the appetizer, simply increase the heat under the wok to the highest setting and complete the stir-fry in seconds.

Szechwan Chicken

SERVES 4 TO 10

Because of its higher fat content, chicken thigh meat tastes more succulent than the breast meat. Ask the butcher to do the boning and skinning for you.

4 large heads Belgian endive, as accompaniment
$^1\!/_2$ pound chicken thigh meat, already boned and skinned
3 cloves garlic, finely minced
1 whole green onion, minced
1 tablespoon finely minced ginger
2 tablespoons hoisin sauce
1 tablespoon oyster sauce
1 tablespoon white or red wine vinegar
1 tablespoon dark sesame oil
1 tablespoon Asian chile sauce
2 tablespoons flavorless cooking oil

Separate the endive cups and set aside. Cut the chicken into $^1\!/_4$-inch-square cubes. Place the chicken in a bowl and add all of the remaining ingredients except the cooking oil. Mix thoroughly and refrigerate. *The recipe can be completed to this point up to 8 hours before cooking.*

Place a wok or sauté pan over high heat until very hot. Add the cooking oil and roll it around the sides of the wok. When the oil just begins to smoke, add the chicken mixture. Stir and toss until the chicken pieces are cooked through, about 90 seconds. Slide the stir-fry onto a heated platter. Surround with endive cups and serve at once.

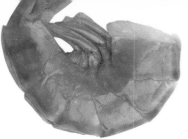

Thai Spicy Beef with Boston Lettuce

SERVES 4 TO 10

Toasted nuts and the rich sweetness of hoisin heighten the flavor of the beef in this recipe. Be sure to ask the butcher to trim all the silver skin from the piece of tenderloin.

1/2 pound beef tenderloin, trimmed of all fat and silver skin
2 tablespoons hoisin sauce
1 tablespoon dry sherry
1/4 cup pine nuts or slivered almonds
2 whole small green onions, minced
3 cloves garlic, finely minced
1 head Boston or Bibb lettuce, or 4 large heads Belgian endive, as accompaniment
2 tablespoons flavorless cooking oil

WOK SAUCE
2 tablespoons thick coconut milk (from the top of the can)
2 tablespoons Thai or Vietnamese fish sauce or thin soy sauce
1 tablespoon light brown sugar
1 tablespoon Asian chile sauce
1 teaspoon cornstarch
2 tablespoons chopped fresh mint
2 tablespoons chopped fresh basil

Cut the beef crosswise in 1/8-inch slices, then cut the slices into shreds. In a large bowl, mix together the hoisin and dry sherry. Add the beef, stir to coat, and refrigerate. Preheat the oven to 325°. Spread the nuts on a baking sheet and toast in the oven until golden, 8 to 10 minutes. Combine the green onions and garlic. Tear the lettuce leaves into 16 small cups, or separate the endive leaves. In a small bowl, stir together the sauce ingredients and refrigerate. *The recipe can be completed to this point up to 8 hours before cooking.*

Place a wok or sauté pan over high heat until very hot. Add the cooking oil and roll it around the sides of the wok. When the oil just begins to smoke, add the beef and stir-fry. As soon as the beef's outside raw color disappears (about 30 seconds), add the green onions and garlic. Stir-fry for 15 seconds. Stir the sauce in its bowl and add the sauce to the stir-fry. Add the nuts. Stir and toss until the sauce glazes the beef. Slide the stir-fry onto a heated platter. Surround with lettuce cups and serve at once.

Stir-Fry Shrimp in Endive Cups

SERVES 4 TO 10

Stir-frying shrimp in this rich, spicy sauce accented with ginger and cilantro perfectly matches the slight bitterness of the endive cup. It's important to cut the shrimp crosswise into very thin slices so the pieces will fit neatly into the lettuce cups. See photograph, page 99.

1/2 pound medium raw shrimp, shelled and deveined, or bay scallops
2 whole small green onions, minced
2 tablespoons finely minced ginger
4 large heads Belgian endive, as accompaniment
2 tablespoons flavorless cooking oil

WOK SAUCE
2 tablespoons chopped fresh cilantro sprigs
2 tablespoons oyster sauce
2 tablespoons dry sherry
1 tablespoon dark sesame oil
2 teaspoons hot sauce or Asian chile sauce
1/2 teaspoon sugar
1/2 teaspoon cornstarch

Cut the shrimp crosswise in paper-thin "rounds" and refrigerate. Combine the green onions and ginger and refrigerate. Cut ends off endive, separate leaves, and refrigerate. In a small bowl, stir together the sauce ingredients and refrigerate. *The recipe can be completed to this point up to 8 hours before cooking.*

Place a wok or sauté pan over high heat until very hot. Add the cooking oil and roll it around the sides of the wok. When the oil just begins to smoke, add the shrimp. Stir-fry the shrimp. As soon as the shrimp turn white (about 45 seconds), add the green onions and ginger. Stir the sauce and add it to the stir-fry. Stir and toss until the sauce glazes the shrimp. Slide the stir-fry onto a heated platter. Surround with endive cups and serve at once.

Spicy Thai Ground Lamb with Seared Tortillas

SERVES 4 TO 10

Ground meat makes a wonderful filling for lettuce cups. We prefer lamb because of its rich taste, but also use ground beef, veal, and pork. Ground chicken and turkey, because of their low fat content, create rather tasteless fillings.

½ pound ground lamb
1 tablespoon hoisin sauce
1 tablespoon Thai or Vietnamese fish sauce or oyster sauce
1 tablespoon freshly squeezed lime juice
1 tablespoon Asian chile sauce
3 cloves garlic, finely minced
6 (6-inch) flour tortillas
2 tablespoons flavorless cooking oil
¼ cup fresh basil, chopped
¼ cup fresh mint, chopped

In a large bowl, combine the lamb, hoisin sauce, fish sauce, lime juice, chile sauce, and garlic. Using your hands, mix thoroughly, then refrigerate. Lightly brown the tortillas by placing them directly over a gas stove burner turned to high, on an indoor or outdoor grill, or in an ungreased frying pan. Leave the tortillas whole or cut into quarters. Stack, wrap with foil, and set aside. *The recipe can be completed to this point up to 8 hours before cooking.*

Preheat the oven to 325°. Warm the foil-wrapped tortillas in the oven for about 8 minutes. Place a wok or sauté pan over high heat until very hot. Add the cooking oil and roll it around the sides of the wok. When the oil just begins to smoke, add the lamb. Stir-fry the lamb, pressing it against the sides of the wok to break it up. When the lamb just loses its raw color, stir in the herbs. Slide the stir-fry onto a heated platter and surround with the tortillas. Serve immediately.

From left: Spicy Thai Ground Lamb with Seared Tortillas, Stir-Fry Shrimp in Endive Cups (page 97)

Asian Dumplings and Spring Rolls

These recipes don't look fast, but they are! Just mince the filling in a food processor hours in advance. When your dinner guests arrive, gather them around the kitchen table to help fold the dumplings. You'll be amazed how everyone enjoys being a part of the culinary action! Of course, the dumplings can be folded hours ahead. But if you want a fast appetizer and your friends aren't going to help with the folding, choose a recipe from another chapter in this book.

Southwest Pan-Fried Lamb Dumplings with Salsa

SERVES 6 TO 10

If vine-ripened tomatoes are not in season, replace the salsa with the Coconut-Herb Glaze (page 101) or the Spicy Orange Glaze (page 101).

1 tablespoon finely minced ginger
2 whole green onions
$^3/_4$ pound ground lamb, veal, or pork, or finely minced
    raw shrimp
1 tablespoon thin or low-sodium soy sauce
30 wonton skins, thinnest type
$^1/_4$ cup cornstarch
2 tablespoons flavorless cooking oil

SALSA
$^2/_3$ cup seeded and finely chopped vine-ripened tomatoes
$^1/_3$ cup chicken broth
1 tablespoon oyster sauce
2 teaspoons Asian chile sauce or hot sauce
1 whole green onion, minced
3 tablespoons minced fresh cilantro sprigs
1 clove garlic, finely minced

To prepare the filling, mince the ginger and green onions separately in the food processor, then place in a bowl. Add the lamb and soy sauce and, using your hands, mix thoroughly. Refrigerate.

Trim the wontons into $2^1/_2$-inch-diameter circles; cover tightly with plastic wrap and refrigerate. In a bowl, combine all of the sauce ingredients and refrigerate.

Fold dumplings and cook following the directions for the Pan-Fried Scallop Dumplings on page 101.

Pan-Fried Scallop Dumplings with Coconut-Herb Glaze

SERVES 6 TO 10

The key to cooking these dumplings is to have a nonstick skillet to guarantee that the dumplings will slide out effortlessly every time. Test to see if the dumplings are cooked by pressing them with your index finger during the cooking. The moment the dumplings become firm to the touch, they are fully cooked. See photograph, page 105.

1 tablespoon finely minced ginger
2 whole green onions
1/4 pound raw medium shrimp, shelled and deveined
1/2 pound fresh sea scallops, shrimp, salmon fillet, or
    ground meat
1 tablespoon thin or low-sodium soy sauce
30 wonton skins, thinnest type
1/4 cup cornstarch
2 tablespoons flavorless cooking oil

COCONUT-HERB GLAZE
1/2 cup unsweetened coconut milk
1/2 cup freshly squeezed orange juice
1 tablespoon oyster sauce
1/2 teaspoon Indian curry powder
1/2 teaspoon Asian chile sauce or hot sauce
2 tablespoons minced fresh basil or cilantro sprigs

To prepare the filling, mince the ginger, green onion, shrimp, and scallops separately in the food processor, then place in a bowl. Add the soy sauce and, using your hands, mix thoroughly. Refrigerate. Trim the wontons into 2 1/2-inch circles; cover tightly with plastic wrap and refrigerate. In a bowl, combine the sauce ingredients and refrigerate.

To make the dumplings, place a wonton skin on a flat surface. Place 2 teaspoons of filling in the center. Bring the edges of the skin up around the filling. Encircle the dumpling "waist" with your index finger and thumb, while flattening the top and the bottom of the dumpling using your other hand. Repeat with the remaining ingredients. Transfer to a baking sheet lined with parchment paper and dusted heavily with cornstarch. Refrigerate.

The dumplings can be completed to this point up to 12 hours before cooking; or they can be frozen on a sheet pan, transfered to a zip-top bag, and kept for up to 3 months in the freezer.

If the dumplings are frozen, do not defrost. Place a 12-inch non-stick sauté pan over high heat. Add the cooking oil, then immediately place the dumplings, bottom side down, into the pan. Fry the dumplings until the bottoms are golden brown, about 2 minutes. Pour in the sauce. Immediately cover the pan, reduce the heat to medium-high, and cook the dumplings until firm to the touch (about 30 seconds if fresh and 90 seconds if frozen). Remove the lid and shake the pan so that the dumplings "cap-size" and are glazed all over with the sauce. Transfer the dumplings to a heated serving platter and serve at once, with toothpicks if desired.

Spicy Orange Glaze for Dumplings

MAKES 1 CUP

Changing the sauce radically changes the flavor of the dumplings. Substitute this sauce in either of the previous two dumpling recipes.

2/3 cup freshly squeezed orange or tangerine juice
1/4 cup dry sherry
1 tablespoon oyster sauce
1 to 2 teaspoons Asian chile sauce
1 whole green onion, minced
1 tablespoon finely minced ginger
1 clove garlic, finely minced

Combine all of the ingredients in a small bowl. *The glaze will keep for up to 24 hours in the refrigerator.*

Shrimp Dumplings with Chinese Pesto

SERVES 6 TO 12

Serve these dumplings when you want to keep cooking to a minimum. The dumplings are simply boiled, drained, and tossed in a spicy sauce.

2 whole green onions
3/4 pound raw medium shrimp, shelled and deveined
1 tablespoon oyster sauce
2 teaspoons dry sherry
1 tablespoon white sesame seeds
30 wonton skins, thinnest type
1/4 cup cornstarch

CHINESE PESTO
2 cups spinach leaves, washed and dried and loosely packed
1/4 cup fresh cilantro sprigs
8 leaves fresh basil
1 clove garlic, chopped
2 tablespoons finely minced ginger
1/2 teaspoon grated orange zest
1/4 cup freshly squeezed orange juice
2 tablespoons white or red wine vinegar
2 tablespoons dark sesame oil
1 tablespoon thin or low-sodium soy sauce
2 teaspoons hoisin sauce
1/2 teaspoon Asian chile sauce

To prepare the filling, mince the green onions and shrimp separately in the food processor, then place in a bowl. Add the oyster sauce and sherry and, using your hands, mix thoroughly. Refrigerate.

In an ungreased skillet over high heat, toast the sesame seeds until golden. Set aside.

To make the dumplings, trim the wonton skins into 2 1/2-inch circles. Place a wonton skin on a flat surface. Place 2 teaspoons of filling in the center, moisten the edges with water, fold the dumpling in half over the filling, and press together to seal. Moisten one end of the dumpling, then touch the ends and pinch together. The dumpling should look like a little cap. Repeat with the remaining wontons. Transfer to a baking sheet lined with parchment paper and dusted heavily with cornstarch. Refrigerate uncovered. *The dumplings can be completed to this point up to 12 hours before cooking; or they can be frozen on a sheet pan, transfered to a zip-top bag, and kept for up to 3 months in the freezer.*

To prepare the pesto, place all of the pesto ingredients in a blender and liquefy. Transfer to a small bowl and refrigerate. *The sauce can be made up to 12 hours before cooking.*

To cook the dumplings, bring 5 quarts of water to a vigorous boil. Add the dumplings and give them a gentle stir. Cook until all the dumplings float to the surface, about 3 minutes. Gently drain the dumplings in a colander, then transfer to a large bowl. Add the pesto and toss. Transfer the dumplings to a heated serving platter, sprinkle on the sesame seeds, and serve at once.

Crisp Salmon Spring Rolls with Lettuce Cup Wraps

SERVES 6 TO 10

It's the double frying that gives these spring rolls such a crisp skin. Unfortunately, the frying has to be done just before serving. We do this in a heavy 14-inch skillet placed on the outdoor gas barbecue, so that the house has no oil smell. And because of the last-minute work, we never double the recipe to serve a larger group and instead choose another appetizer. Spring roll skins are tissue-thin sheets available in Asian markets and always sold frozen. Look for Menlo Wrappers or Spring Home Wrappers.

2 tablespoons finely minced ginger
2 whole green onions
³/₄ pound salmon fillet
1 tablespoon grated lemon zest
1 tablespoon oyster sauce
7 spring roll skins, 8 by 8 inches,
    or 14 spring roll skins, 4 ¹/₂ by 4 ¹/₂ inches
2 eggs, well beaten
1 head Bibb lettuce
14 mint leaves
2 cups flavorless cooking oil
One or more dipping sauces (pages 16–22)

Mince the ginger, green onions, and salmon separately in the food processor, then place in a bowl. Add the lemon zest and oyster sauce and, using your hands, mix well.

If using the 8 by 8-inch spring roll skins, cut the spring rolls in half on the diagonal. Working on a flat surface, place a spring roll skin so that one of the corners is pointing at you. Distribute about ¹/₄ cup of the filling along the bottom third of the skin. Bring the corner pointing at you over the filling. Roll the spring roll half a turn. Brush the edges of the skin with beaten egg, fold them in, and roll the spring roll into a cylinder. Repeat with the remaining ingredients. Transfer the spring rolls to a baking sheet lined with parchment paper. Refrigerate uncovered. Do not freeze.

Prepare a dipping sauce. Tear the lettuce into 14 (4 by 4-inch) cups. Refrigerate the lettuce and mint leaves. *The recipe can be completed to this point up to 12 hours before cooking.*

To cook the spring rolls, heat the oil in a 12- or 14-inch sauté pan over high heat until the tip of a wooden chopstick or wooden spoon bubbles when placed in the oil. Fry the spring rolls, turning once, until very light golden, about 30 seconds. Drain on a wire rack.

Continue to heat the oil until it is very hot, but not so hot that it smokes. Fry the spring rolls a second time, turning once, until golden brown. Drain momentarily on a wire rack.

To serve, transfer the spring rolls to a heated platter and accompany with the dipping sauce, lettuce leaves, and mint. To eat, wrap the spring rolls with mint and lettuce cups, and dip into the sauce.

From top: Crisp Salmon Spring Rolls with Lettuce Cup Wraps, Pan-Fried Scallop Dumplings with Coconut-Herb Glaze (page 101), Sweet-and-Sour Apricot Dip (page 17), Mango Salsa (page 18)

Chiles, ancho: These reddish-purple dried chiles have a fruity, mildly spicy taste. They are sold in all Mexican markets and in American supermarkets that have a wide selection of dry chiles. Substitute: dried mulato or pasilla chiles.

Chiles, fresh: The smaller the chile, the spicier its taste. Because it is a tedious operation to remove the seeds from jalapeño and serrano chiles, we always mince the chiles including their seeds by using an electric mini-chopper. Substitute: your favorite bottled chile sauce.

Chipotle chiles in adobo sauce: These spicy chiles are smoked, dried jalapeños (chipotle chiles) stewed in a tomato-vinegar-garlic sauce (adobo sauce). Available in 4-ounce cans at all Mexican markets and many supermarkets. To use, purée the chiles with the adobo sauce in an electric mini-chopper. It is unnecessary to remove the seeds. Substitute: none.

Citrus juice: Freshly squeezed citrus juice has a sparkling "fresh" taste completely absent in all storebought juices. Because its flavor deteriorates quickly, always squeeze citrus juice within hours of use and keep refrigerated.

Citrus zest: The colored skin of citrus, removed using the simple tool pictured on page 12.

Coconut milk: Adds flavor and body to sauces. Always purchase a Thai brand whose ingredients are just coconut and water. Do not buy the new "low-calorie" coconut milk, which has a terrible taste. Stir the coconut milk before using. Best brand: Chaokoh Brand from Thailand. Once opened, store coconut milk in the refrigerator for up to 1 week, then discard. Substitute: half-and-half or chicken broth.

Cooking oil: Use any flavorless oil that has a high smoking temperature, such as peanut oil, canola oil, safflower oil, or corn oil.

Fish sauce, Thai or Vietnamese: Made from fermenting fish in brine and used in Southeast Asian cooking to add a complex flavor in much the same way that the Chinese use soy sauce. Purchase Thai fish sauce, which has the lowest salt content. Best brands: Three Crab Brand, Phu Quoc Flying Lion Brand, or Tiparos Brand Fish Sauce. Substitute: thin soy sauce, although the flavor is quite different.

Anchovy paste: An anchovy purée mixed with spices and sold in 2-ounce tubes by most supermarkets. Keeps indefinitely if refrigerated.

Capers: Small buds picked from a type of bush common in the Mediterranean. Capers are packed in brine and sold bottled. Once opened, they last indefinitely if refrigerated and kept covered by their liquid. Rinse before using.

Cheese (Parmesan, Pecorino, and Asiago): Use these three cheeses interchangeably. Because of their unrivaled flavor, make an extra effort to locate these Italian cheeses at upscale supermarkets and cheese shops. As long as the cheese has not been grated, it will last at least 1 month wrapped airtight and refrigerated.

Chile sauce, Asian: A general term for the countless varieties of chile sauces imported from Asia added to provide "heat" to the food, use your own favorite chile sauce and vary the amount depending on personal preference. Best brand: Rooster Brand Delicious Hot Chili Garlic Sauce, sold in 8-ounce clear plastic jars with a green cap. Refrigerate after opening. Substitute: one or more fresh jalapeño or serrano chiles.

Five-spice powder: A blend of anise, fennel, cinnamon, cloves, and Szechwan pepper. Sold at all Asian markets and in the spice section of most supermarkets.

Ginger, fresh: These pungent and spicy "roots" grown in Hawaii are available at all supermarkets in the produce section. Buy firm ginger with a smooth skin. It is unnecessary to peel ginger unless the skin is wrinkled. To use: Rinse well. Because the tough ginger fiber runs lengthwise along the root, always cut the ginger crosswise in paper-thin slices, then very finely mince in an electric mini-chopper. Store ginger in the refrigerator. There is no substitute for fresh ginger.

Hoisin sauce: A thick, sweet, spicy, dark condiment made with soy beans, chiles, garlic, ginger, and sugar. Once opened, it keeps indefinitely at room temperature. Best brand: Koon Chun.

Olive oil, extra virgin: Although "extra virgin" is the most expensive type of olive oil, its rich flavor is a necessary component in the recipes that specify this type of oil.

Olives, kalamata: Dark purple, rich, and fruity tasting, these and other olives from Europe are utterly different and far superior to the dreadful American canned olives. European olives are sold in the deli section of most supermarkets.

Oyster sauce: Also called "oyster-flavored sauce," this sauce gives dishes a complex taste without a hint of its seafood origins. Keeps indefinitely in the refrigerator. There is no substitute. The following brands are available mostly at Asian markets: Sa Cheng Oyster Flavored Sauce, Hop Sing Lung Oyster Sauce, and Lee Kum Kee Oyster Flavored Sauce, Premium Brand. Asian markets also sell vegetarian oyster sauce.

Plum sauce: Made from plums, apricots, garlic, chiles, sugar, and vinegar, and available bottled at all Asian markets and most supermarkets. Best brand: Koon Chun. It will keep indefinitely if stored in the refrigerator.

Red peppers, roasted: These are sweet red bell peppers that are roasted and then peeled and seeded. They are available bottled and are sold alongside pickles and relishes at every supermarket.

Sesame oil, dark: A nutty, dark golden brown oil made from toasted crushed sesame seeds. Do not confuse dark sesame oil with the American-manufactured clear-colored and flavorless sesame oil or Chinese black sesame oil, which has a strong unpleasant taste. Dark sesame oil will last for at least a year at room temperature, and indefinitely in the refrigerator. Best brand: Kadoya.

Sesame seeds, white: Use the pure white sesame seeds sold in the spice section of every supermarket, not the inferior-tasting light brown sesame seeds from Japan.

Sherry, dry: Use any moderately priced dry sherry, or substitute any Japanese or Chinese rice wine, or dry vermouth.

Soy sauce, dark: Dark, "heavy" or "black" soy sauce is slightly thicker (molasses or caramel is added) than thin soy sauce and has a richer flavor. Do not confuse dark soy sauce with "thick" soy sauce, which is an overwhelmingly powerful-tasting syrup.

Soy sauce, thin: "Thin" or "light" soy sauce is a "watery," mildly salty liquid made from soy beans, roasted wheat, yeast, and salt. Best brands: Pearl River Bridge Brand Golden Label Superior Soy Sauce, Koon Chun Brand Thin Soy Sauce, Kikkoman Regular Soy Sauce, or a low-sodium soy sauce.

Vinegar, balsamic: This vinegar has a complex, nutty, mildly sour, slightly sweet flavor. For recipes in this book, use the moderately priced balsamic vinegar ($5 for an 8-ounce bottle) available at most supermarkets.

Vinegar, rice: The mild flavor of Japanese rice vinegar is a great addition to salads. "Seasoned" or "gourmet" rice vinegar has sugar added.

Acknowledgments

Many friends helped bring this book into print, and we are deeply appreciative for your support and many contributions. Thank you Ten Speed Press, particularly Phil Wood, our publisher Kirsty Melville, and Jo Ann Deck and Dennis Hayes in special sales, who urged us to do this book. Many thanks also to our editor Chelsea Vaughn who did a wonderful job molding the book into its final form, and to copyeditor Jenny Morrison, who had scores of useful suggestions. Our friend and book designer Beverly Wilson contributed her unique vision for the book and added so much to our pleasure working on this book. Joanna Cantrall helped with recipe testing and food styling of the photographs, as did food stylist Carol Cole, who added her special talents. Jack and Dolores Cakebread provided their winery kitchen for testing many of these recipes with a small group of cooking friends. Thank you all—it was wonderful to work with you on this exciting book.

Artists' Credits

We would especially like to thank our contributing artists and galleries. Versatile ceramic artist Julie Sanders, of the Cyclamen Collection, Emeryville, California, made the graceful and colorful dishes on pages 5, 10, 23, 43, 51, 55, 61, 71, and 95. Kathy Erteman of New York City made the graphic black-and-white wares on pages 1, 7, 34, 79, and 103. Julie Cline of Oakland, California, made the hand-painted dishes on page 27. Vineware made the plate on page 38. Barbara Eigen made the square plates on pages 74–75.

Glass artist Paul Hathcoat of the Hathcoat Studios, Ltd., in Colorado Springs, Colorado, made the colorful glass plates on page 42 and 85 and the platters on pages 98 and 99.

Glass artist Stephen Smyers of Smyers Glass, Inc., in Benicia, California, made the beautiful dishes on page 46, the glasses on pages 19 and 82, and the glasses and coasters on page 71. Debbie Young of Escondido, California, made the fused glass platter on page 58.

ZIA Houseworks, Berkeley, California, was our source for the Susan Eslick bowls and the DYOA platter on page 19. ZIA also lent us the Annie Glass heart plates and DYOA platters on pages 29 and 49, and the Rosenwold Botanical plate on page 82. They were our source for the Kathy Erteman black-and-white platters and the wire basket on page 34, and the Kathy Erteman platter on page 79. ZIA also represents the Luna Garcia plates on page 89 and the Duex Amies Davis Bull's-eye dishes on page 105.

R.S. Basso of St. Helena, California, was the source for the wire basket on page 43, the fabric and candlesticks on page 46, the pedestal on page 58, and the accessories on pages 82 and 98–99.

Fillamento Gallery of San Francisco, California, was the source for the Japanese wares on page 65.

We salute all these talented artists, and thank you all for being a part of *Fast Appetizers*!

Conversion Charts

Liquid Measurements

Cups and Spoons	Fluid Ounces	Approximate Metric Term	Approximate Centiliters	Actual Milliliters
1 tsp	⅙ oz	*	½ cL	5 mL
1 Tb	½ oz	*	1½ cL	15 mL
¼ c	2 oz	½ dL	6 cL	59 mL
⅓ c	2⅔ oz	¾ dL	8 cL	79 mL
½ c	4 oz	1 dL	12 cL	119 mL
⅔ c	5⅓ oz	1½ dL	15 cL	157 mL
¾ c	6 oz	1¾ dL	18 cL	178 mL
1 c	8 oz	¼ L	24 cL	237 mL
1¼ c	10 oz	3 dL	30 cL	296 mL
1⅓ c	10⅔ oz	3¼ dL	33 cL	325 mL
1½ c	12 oz	3½ dL	35 cL	355 mL
1⅔ c	13⅓ oz	3¾ dL	39 cL	385 mL
1¾ c	14 oz	4 dL	41 cL	414 mL
2 c; 1 pt	16 oz	½ L	47 cL	473 mL
2½ c	20 oz	6 dL	60 cL	592 mL
3 c	24 oz	¾ L	70 cL	710 mL
3½ c	28 oz	⅘ L	83 cL	829 mL
4 c	32 oz	1 L	95 cL	946 mL
5 c	40 oz	1¼ L	113 cL	1134 mL
6 c	48 oz	1½ L	142 cL	1420 mL
8 c	64 oz	2 L	190 cL	1893 mL
10 c	80 oz	2½ L	235 cL	2366 mL
12 c	96 oz	2¾ L	284 cL	2839 mL
4 qt	128 oz	3¾ L	375 cL	3785 mL
5 qt	160 oz			
6 qt	192 oz			
8 qt	256 oz			

* Metric equivalent too small for home measure.

Length

⅛ in = 3 mm
¼ in = 6 mm
⅓ in = 1 cm
½ in = 1.5 cm
¾ in = 2 cm
1 in = 2.5 cm
1½ in = 4 cm
2 in = 5 cm
2½ in = 6 cm
4 in = 10 cm
8 in = 20 cm
10 in = 25 cm

Temperatures

275˚F = 140˚C
300˚F = 150˚C
325˚F = 170˚C
350˚F = 180˚C
375˚F = 190˚C
400˚F = 200˚C
425˚F = 215˚C
450˚F = 230˚C
475˚F = 240˚C
500˚F = 250˚C

Other Conversions

Ounces to milliliters: multiply ounces by 29.57

Quarts to liters: multiply quarts by 0.95

Milliliters to ounces: multiply milliliters by 0.034

Liters to quarts: multiply liters by 1.057

Ounces to grams: multiply ounces by 28.3

Grams to ounces: multiply grams by .0353

Pounds to grams: multiply pounds by 453.59

Pounds to kilograms: multiply pounds by 0.45

Cups to liters: multiply cups by 0.24

Index

Fifty bold and sophisticated yet easy stir-fry recipes seasoned with a host of exciting ingredients. Perfect ideas for fresh, healthy weeknight meals or weekend entertaining. Includes more than fifty vibrant color photos.

Fifty wild and zesty recipes that combine chicken with the distinct flavors and cuisines of the world. Discover delicious and elegant ways to serve one of the most versatile and healthful meats. More than fifty color photos provide dramatic presentation ideas.

Fifty fresh and sensational recipes take pasta to new and dazzling heights. Packed with easy, inventive ideas, this is the complete resource for busy cooks at all levels of experience. Includes more than fifty exciting color photos.

Fifty sizzling recipes for classic barbecue favorites and innovative pleasers from around the world. From simple any-night delights to elaborate weekend feasts, this tantalizing offering will heat up backyards and kitchens alike.

More of the winning Hot formula: sixty-plus original recipes, organized alphabetically from artichokes to zucchini, introduce a palate-tingling world of veggie-based soups, salads, pastas, sides, and entrées.

Platters of tender, juicy ribs have long reigned as home-cooking favorites. *The Great Ribs Book* brings you the lowdown on the different types of ribs, cooking techniques, sauces, and more. Includes more than 60 recipes pairing ribs with delectable flavors from all over the world.